Betty Crocker
Bisquick II
Cookbook

Betty Crocker
Bisquick II
Cookbook

WILEY

Wiley Publishing, Inc.

Library of Congress Cataloging-in-Publication Data:

Crocker, Betty.
  Betty Crocker bisquick II cookbook : easy, delicious dinners, breakfasts, desserts and more.
      p. cm.
Includes index.
      ISBN 0-7645-4339-3 (Hardcover—Concealed Wir-O : alk. paper)
      1. Cookery, American. 2. Quick and easy cookery. I. Crocker, Betty.
    TX715 .B4888 2004
    641.5'55—dc22
                        2003020610

Manufactured in China
10 9 8 7 6 5 4 3 2

Cover photo: Ultimate Chicken Pot Pie (page 92)

GENERAL MILLS, INC.

Director, Book and On-line Publishing: Kim Walter

Manager, Book Publishing: Lois L. Tlusty

Editor: Cheri A. Olerud

Recipe Development and Testing: Betty Crocker Kitchens

Food Styling: Betty Crocker Kitchens

Photography: General Mills Photo Studios

WILEY PUBLISHING, INC.

Publisher: Natalie Chapman

Executive Editor: Anne Ficklen

Managing Editor: S. Kristi Hart

Editor: Caroline Schleifer

Senior Production Editor: Jennifer Mazurkie

Cover Design: Jeff Faust

Interior Design: Edwin Kuo

Interior Layout: Holly Wittenberg

Manufacturing Manager: Kevin Watt

The Betty Crocker Kitchens seal guarantees success in your kitchen. Every recipe has been tested in America's Most Trusted Kitchens™ to meet our high standards of reliability, easy preparation and great taste.

For more great ideas visit *BettyCrocker*.com

The Joys of Bisquick Mix

What a great idea! It all started back in the 1930s with basic biscuits. Here at last was a mix that made light and tasty biscuits, once a special-occasion bread, easy enough for every day. Since then, Bisquick has become the country's premier convenience baking mix—an all-around ingredient perfect for any meal or occasion. You probably have a box in your kitchen, too.

So what are all the great recipes you can make from this cheerful yellow box? Bisquick makes thousands of quick and easy recipes, from pancakes and biscuits to pizzas, casseroles, Impossibly Easy pies, pot pies and cobblers. When you have a box of Bisquick on your shelf, you're ready at a moment's notice to answer the "What's for dinner?" question. From tried-and-true favorites to new ways to excite and delight your family, Bisquick recipes pave the way to tasty meal ideas.

Whether you need a quick dinner idea, want to enjoy Saturday morning waffles with the family or want to try a fun new holiday recipe, Bisquick makes it easy, fun and, most important, always delicious. So treat your family to Bisquick favorites—the easy way to make every day homemade.

Shirley Dolland

Shirley Dolland
from the Betty Crocker kitchens

CONTENTS

DISCOVER Bisquick Mix

Bisquick is the perfect recipe for creating wonderful family moments. Life can be hectic, demanding and full of compromises. You may not be able to prepare the kind of meals your mother made or the kind of meals you'd like to make if you just had more time. What can make mealtime easier? Bisquick mix contains flour, shortening, baking powder and salt, so it saves you both mixing and measuring time. And because it can be used to make so many recipes, Bisquick is a valuable staple in today's busy world. As long as your pantry is stocked with Bisquick, you don't even need to plan ahead.

So gather your family together and create mealtime experiences they'll always remember. Refuel and reconnect at the same time with food that's tasty, warm and homemade. For breakfast, try Ultimate Best-Ever Waffles (page 33) or Maple-Sour Cream Pancakes (page 22). Your family will love Mini Barbecued Meat Loaves (page 102) or Cheesy Chicken Casserole (page 90) for dinner. And if your kids enjoy helping in the kitchen or even baking all on their own, P B and J Strips (page 228) or Chocolate Waffle Cookies (page 227) are sure to become new favorites. There are plenty of other delicious recipes to try—all of them made easier and quicker with Bisquick.

Not One, But Two Bisquick Cookbooks

You may be wondering why there are two Bisquick cookbooks, and which one to buy. If you like cooking and baking with Bisquick mix, you'll be sure to enjoy both books. The first Bisquick cookbook, with its heritage message and all-time favorite recipes, was a huge hit. Still, consumers are always asking for more Bisquick recipes, so *Bisquick II* was born! In *Bisquick II*, you'll find an easier, more contemporary approach—*new* Bisquick recipes have eight or fewer ingredients, preparation times of 15 minutes or less and a greater focus on main dish recipes. In fact, there's a whole chapter devoted to solving mealtime madness, with recipes that can be prepared in 30 minutes or less. You'll be able to quickly find which recipes kids spark to and can easily make, marked by the Kids Love icon kids ♥ LOVE. In familiar Betty style, there are helpful hints and tips with all the recipes.

You Asked!

Bisquick is easy to use and always makes recipes taste great. But there are still some questions that come up time after time. Here are the top ten most-often-asked questions about Bisquick—from people who buy Bisquick and use it just like you!

Q: How should I measure Bisquick?

A: For best results, spoon Bisquick mix—without sifting—into a dry-ingredient measuring cup and level with a straight-edged knife or spatula. Do not press or tap Bisquick into the cup; it packs too much mix into the cup and will make the dough or batter too heavy.

Q: How should I store Bisquick?

A: To keep Bisquick mix fresh, store it in either the original box, an airtight container or a plastic bag, and store in a cool, dry place like your pantry shelf. If keeping it for a longer time, store it in the refrigerator or freezer for up to 1 year. If frozen, bring it to room temperature before using.

Q: Can Bisquick pancake and waffle batter be prepared ahead?

A: Yes, but not too far ahead. Make the batter, then cover and refrigerate for up to 1 hour. If the batter stands for longer than an hour, your pancakes or waffles may not be as light and puffy.

Q: Can I double the recipes for Impossibly Easy Pies?

A: Sure! Just double the ingredients and bake in two 9-inch pie plates or one 13 × 9-inch baking dish. You may need to increase the baking time slightly if you use the baking dish. Be sure to check the doneness of the pie at the earliest time given in the original recipe.

High Altitude Baking with Bisquick

There are no hard and fast rules to follow when baking with Bisquick at high altitude. Changes depend upon the recipe you are making and the proportion of ingredients. For best results, use recipes—like all of the recipes in this book—that have been tested and adjusted for high altitude. Decreased air pressure at higher altitudes changes the way foods cook and bake. At high altitude, some of the reasons that baked goods may bake differently than at sea level include:

- Gases expand more from the leavening
- Boiling point of liquids decreases
- Evaporation happens at a faster rate

These changes mean that baked goods can sink, collapse or brown too much. Follow the high-altitude adjustments for each recipe, but some common adjustments from the sea-level recipe may include one or more of the following:

- Increasing oven temperature
- Baking for a longer time
- Adding more Bisquick mix
- Also, some recipes may require adding flour or decreasing sugar or oil.

Can I substitute Bisquick in recipes if I run out of flour?

Bisquick mix works just like flour to thicken a stew or gravy or to coat foods before cooking. Use the same amount of Bisquick as you would flour and use the same way. Since Bisquick mix contains more ingredients than flour, such as shortening, baking powder and salt, it's best to follow recipes specifically for baking with Bisquick when you want to use it to make cakes, pies, cookies or other baked goods.

Is Bisquick affected by humidity?

Bisquick mix reacts to the environment just as any flour-based ingredient does. In humid weather, you may find that doughs and batters are more sticky, soft or wet. You can add small amounts of Bisquick to make the dough or batter easier to work with.

Can I use buttermilk in pancakes or waffles?

Yes, just use the same amount of buttermilk as you would milk or water for pancakes or waffles. Buttermilk adds a tangy, rich dairy flavor to baked foods.

What's the best way to store leftover waffles, pancakes and biscuits?

Freshly made waffles, pancakes and biscuits are the best, but it's also a treat to have leftovers to enjoy. If you happen to have any extras, store them in an airtight container or plastic food-storage bag in the refrigerator no longer than 2 days, or freeze for up to 3 months. Reheat waffles by toasting them in your toaster. Microwave individual frozen pancakes or biscuits on High for 20 to 30 seconds.

Can you give me some tips for making the best biscuits?

For soft, tender biscuits, start out by measuring carefully: spoon Bisquick mix lightly into a dry-ingredient measuring cup, then level it off with the edge of a knife or spatula. To measure liquid, place a liquid measuring cup on your counter, pour in the liquid, bend down and check the amount at eye level. When mixing the biscuits, easy does it! Kneading or mixing too long can cause biscuits to become tough. Also, check your oven temperature and baking time; bake biscuits just until golden brown.

Can I use Reduced Fat Bisquick mix in place of Original Bisquick mix?

It depends. Some recipes in this book list both Original and Reduced Fat Bisquick when either one will work. However, because Reduced Fat Bisquick contains less fat, it may work differently in some recipes. The biggest difference is in the amount of water that is absorbed in doughs and batters. For the best results when using Reduced Fat Bisquick mix, try recipes that call for it specifically.

The Ultimate Coating

For a crisp, crunchy breading on chicken, pork chops or fish, there's nothing better than Bisquick. It's a super and versatile coating that you can prepare in less than 5 minutes. It's also easy to add a few extra ingredients for some fun flavor variations. For a basic mix start with:

Impossibly Easy Coating

2/3 cup Original Bisquick mix

1 1/2 teaspoons paprika

1 teaspoon salt

1/4 teaspoon pepper

Mix all ingredients.

Coat:

- 2 1/2 to 3 1/2 pounds cut-up broiler-fryer chicken *or*
- 1 pound fish fillets *or*
- 1 1/4 to 1 1/2 pounds pork chops

Heat oven to 425°. Melt 1 tablespoon butter or margarine in 13 × 9 × 2-inch baking dish. Add coated chicken, fish or pork chops.

Bake:

- Chicken for 50 minutes, turning after 35 minutes, until juice is no longer pink when centers of thickest pieces are cut.
- Fish for 25 to 30 minutes or until fish flakes easily with fork.
- Pork chops for 50 minutes, turning after 25 minutes, until bone-in chops are slightly pink when cut near bone or until boneless chops are slightly pink in center.

Top Tips for Pancakes and Waffles

Light, fluffy and tender, a stack of pancakes or a batch of fresh-baked waffles make a great start to the day. For the best, follow these tips:

- Measure ingredients carefully (see how to measure Bisquick mix and liquids, page 10). Too much liquid will result in a thin batter, and too little liquid will make a batter that is too thick.
- Heat griddle about 5 minutes before you plan to cook pancakes so it has time to reach the right temperature for cooking. To test if the griddle is ready, sprinkle it with a few drops of water. If the drops bounce around, the temperature is just right. When using a waffle iron, check the recommended temperature in the manufacturer's directions and heat the waffle iron to that temperature.
- Cook pancakes only until they're dry around the edges—usually just over a minute—then flip and cook until the other side is golden brown. (Don't flip pancakes more than once, or they may become tough.)
- Cook each waffle just until steaming stops, then open the lid and check waffle to see if it has browned.

Asian Coating: Omit paprika and pepper. Mix in 3 tablespoons sesame seed, 1 tablespoon grated lemon peel, 1 tablespoon soy sauce and 1 1/2 teaspoons garlic powder.

Herb Coating: Add 1 tablespoon each chopped fresh basil, parsley and rosemary leaves.

Italian Coating: Add 1 tablespoon Italian seasoning and 1/2 teaspoon garlic powder.

Mexican Coating: Decrease Bisquick mix to 1/2 cup. Add 2 tablespoons cornmeal, 1 to 2 tablespoons chili powder and 1/2 teaspoon chopped fresh cilantro.

Chapter 1

BREAKFASTS
and Brunches

**Easy Blueberry-Lemon Coffee Cake (page 21)
and Coconut, Pineapple and Macadamia Scones (page 17)**

Orange-Almond Streusel Muffins

PREP: 15 MIN; BAKE: 15 MIN

12 muffins

Streusel Topping (below)

1 teaspoon grated orange peel

1/2 cup orange juice

1/3 cup packed brown sugar

1/4 cup vegetable oil

1 egg

2 cups Original Bisquick mix

1/4 cup sliced almonds

Streusel Topping

1 tablespoon Original Bisquick
mix

2 tablespoons packed brown
sugar

2 tablespoons sliced almonds

1 tablespoon butter or margarine

1. Heat oven to 400°. Line 12 medium muffin cups, 2 1/2 × 1 1/4 inches, with paper baking cups; or grease bottoms only of muffin cups with shortening. Make Streusel Topping; set aside.

2. Mix orange peel, orange juice, brown sugar, oil and egg in large bowl. Stir in Bisquick mix just until moistened. Stir in almonds. Divide batter evenly among muffin cups. Sprinkle with topping.

3. Bake 13 to 15 minutes or until golden brown. Immediately remove from pan to wire rack. Serve warm.

Streusel Topping

Mix Bisquick mix, brown sugar and almonds in medium bowl. Cut in butter, using fork, until crumbly.

High Altitude (3500 to 6500 feet): Use 3/4 cup orange juice and 2 tablespoons oil. Bake 14 to 16 minutes.

Betty's **TIP:** Serve these muffins warm with honey butter or cream cheese. Add fresh fruit and hot tea for a light breakfast, brunch or snack.

1 Muffin: Calories 190 (Calories from Fat 90); Fat 10g (Saturated 2g); Cholesterol 20mg; Sodium 310mg; Carbohydrate 22g (Dietary Fiber 1g); Protein 3g • % **Daily Value:** Vitamin A 0%; Vitamin C 2%; Calcium 4%; Iron 6% • **Exchanges:** 1 Starch, 1/2 Other Carbohydrate, 2 Fat • **Carbohydrate Choices:** 1 1/2

Orange-Almond Streusel Muffins

kids LOVE

Apple-Cheddar Muffins
PREP: 12 MIN; BAKE: 19 MIN

12 muffins

1 egg

2 cups Original Bisquick mix

3/4 cup coarsely chopped peeled
    cooking apple

2/3 cup shredded Cheddar cheese

1/3 cup sugar

2/3 cup milk

2 tablespoons vegetable oil

1 teaspoon ground cinnamon

1. Heat oven to 400°. Line 12 medium muffin cups, 2 1/2 × 1 1/4 inches, with paper baking cups; or grease bottoms only of muffin cups with shortening.

2. Beat egg slightly in medium bowl. Stir in remaining ingredients just until moistened. Divide batter evenly among cups.

3. Bake 17 to 19 minutes or until golden brown. Immediately remove from pan to wire rack. Serve warm.

High Altitude (3500 to 6500 feet): Line muffin cups with paper baking cups.

Betty's **TIP:** These muffins are wonderful for breakfast or as a dinner bread. To rewarm in the microwave, place muffins on a microwavable plate or in a napkin-lined basket and microwave uncovered on High 10 to 15 seconds for 2 muffins or 20 to 30 seconds for 4 muffins.

1 Muffin: Calories 165 (Calories from Fat 65); Fat 7g (Saturated 3g); Cholesterol 10mg; Sodium 330mg; Carbohydrate 20g (Dietary Fiber 1g); Protein 3g • **% Daily Value:** Vitamin A 2%; Vitamin C 0%; Calcium 8%; Iron 4% • **Exchanges:** 1 Starch, 2 Fat • **Carbohydrate Choices:** 1

Coconut, Pineapple and Macadamia Scones

PREP: 10 MIN; BAKE: 14 MIN

Photo on page 12

12 scones

2 1/2 cups Original Bisquick mix

1/4 cup sugar

1/4 cup firm butter or margarine

1/2 cup flaked coconut

1/2 cup chopped macadamia nuts

1/4 cup whipping (heavy) cream

1 egg

1 can (8 ounces) pineapple tidbits, well drained

1. Heat oven to 425°. Spray cookie sheet with cooking spray. Mix Bisquick mix and sugar in large bowl. Cut in butter, using pastry blender or crisscrossing 2 knives, until crumbly. Stir in remaining ingredients.

2. Pat dough into 10-×-7-inch rectangle on cookie sheet (if dough is sticky, dip fingers in Bisquick mix). Cut into 12 rectangles, but do not separate. Sprinkle with additional sugar and coconut if desired.

3. Bake 12 to 14 minutes or until golden brown; carefully separate scones. Serve warm.

High Altitude (3500 to 6500 feet): Bake 14 to 16 minutes.

Betty's **TIP:** Crazy for nuts? Try substituting pecans or almonds for the macadamia nuts, or use a combination of nuts in this tropical scone.

1 Scone: Calories 240 (Calories from Fat 125); Fat 14g (Saturated 6g); Cholesterol 35mg; Sodium 410mg; Carbohydrate 25g (Dietary Fiber 1g); Protein 3g • **% Daily Value:** Vitamin A 4%; Vitamin C 0%; Calcium 6%; Iron 6% • **Exchanges:** 1 Starch, 1/2 Fruit, 3 Fat • **Carbohydrate Choices:** 1 1/2

Cinnamon Bubble Loaf

PREP: 10 MIN; BAKE: 30 MIN; STAND: 10 MIN

1 loaf (12 slices)

2 tablespoons granulated sugar

1 1/2 teaspoons ground cinnamon

3 1/2 cups Original or Reduced Fat Bisquick mix

1/2 cup milk

1/3 cup granulated sugar

3 tablespoons butter or margarine, softened

1 teaspoon vanilla

1 egg

2 tablespoons butter or margarine, melted

Powdered Sugar Glaze (below)

Powdered Sugar Glaze

1/2 cup powdered sugar

2 to 3 teaspoons water

1. Heat oven to 375°. Grease bottom and sides of loaf pan, 9 × 5 × 3 inches, with shortening or spray with cooking spray. Mix 2 tablespoons sugar and the cinnamon; set aside.

2. Stir Bisquick mix, milk, 1/3 cup sugar, 3 tablespoons butter, the vanilla and egg in medium bowl until soft dough forms. Shape dough into 1-inch balls; roll in cinnamon-sugar. Place dough randomly in pan. Sprinkle with any remaining cinnamon-sugar; drizzle melted butter over dough balls.

3. Bake 25 to 30 minutes or until golden brown. Let stand in pan 10 minutes. Remove from pan to wire rack. Make Powdered Sugar Glaze; drizzle over loaf. Cut into slices. Serve warm.

Powdered Sugar Glaze
Mix ingredients until thin enough to drizzle.

High Altitude (3500 to 6500 feet): Bake 33 to 38 minutes.

Betty's **TIP:** Let the kids help! Mix the sugar and cinnamon in a plastic food-storage bag, and have the little ones shake pieces of dough in the mixture. This yummy bread makes a great breakfast after a sleepover—orange juice, bananas and grapes complete the meal.

1 Slice: Calories 240 (Calories from Fat 90); Fat 10g (Saturated 4g); Cholesterol 30mg; Sodium 540mg; Carbohydrate 35g (Dietary Fiber 1g); Protein 3g • **% Daily Value:** Vitamin A 4%; Vitamin C 0%; Calcium 8%; Iron 6% • **Exchanges:** 1 Starch, 1 Other Carbohydrate, 2 Fat • **Carbohydrate Choices:** 2

Cinnamon Bubble Loaf

Raspberry-Banana Oat Bread

PREP: 10 MIN; BAKE: 55 MIN; COOL: 2 HR 10 MIN

1 loaf (24 slices)

2 1/4 cups Original Bisquick mix

2/3 cup sugar

1/3 cup old-fashioned or quick-cooking oats

1 cup mashed very ripe bananas (2 medium)

1/4 cup milk

2 eggs

1 cup fresh or frozen (thawed and drained) raspberries

1. Heat oven to 350°. Grease bottom only of loaf pan, 9 × 5 × 3 inches, with shortening or spray bottom with cooking spray.

2. Stir Bisquick mix, sugar, oats, bananas, milk and eggs in large bowl until moistened; beat vigorously with spoon 30 seconds. Gently stir in raspberries. Pour into pan.

3. Bake 50 to 55 minutes or until toothpick inserted in center comes out clean. Cool 10 minutes. Loosen loaf from sides of pan; remove from pan and place top side up on wire rack. Cool completely, about 2 hours, before slicing.

High Altitude (3500 to 6500 feet): Heat oven to 375°. Use 2 1/2 cups Bisquick mix and 3 eggs.

Betty's **TIP:** To ensure a drier, crisper crust, turn the loaf out of the pan onto a wire rack to cool—if you leave a quick bread in the pan, it will steam and become too soft. This bread will keep up to a week when tightly wrapped and stored in the refrigerator.

1 Slice: Calories 90 (Calories from Fat 20); Fat 2g (Saturated 1g); Cholesterol 20mg; Sodium 170mg; Carbohydrate 16g (Dietary Fiber 1g); Protein 2g • % **Daily Value:** Vitamin A 0%; Vitamin C 2%; Calcium 2%; Iron 2% • **Exchanges:** 1 Starch • **Carbohydrate Choices:** 1

Easy Blueberry-Lemon Coffee Cake

PREP: 10 MIN; BAKE: 25 MIN; COOL: 10 MIN

Photo on page 12

6 to 8 servings

1 egg

2 cups Original Bisquick mix

1/3 cup granulated sugar

2/3 cup milk

1 tablespoon grated lemon peel

1 cup frozen blueberries, thawed, rinsed and well drained

1/4 cup Original Bisquick mix

Lemon Glaze (below)

Lemon Glaze

2/3 cup powdered sugar

3 to 4 teaspoons lemon juice

1. Heat oven to 400°. Grease bottom and side of round pan, 9 × 1 1/2 inches, with shortening or spray with cooking spray. Beat egg slightly in medium bowl. Stir in 2 cups Bisquick mix, the sugar, milk and lemon peel.

2. Mix blueberries and 1/4 cup Bisquick mix; fold into batter. Spread in pan.

3. Bake 20 to 25 minutes or until golden brown. Cool 10 minutes. Drizzle with Lemon Glaze. Serve warm.

Lemon Glaze

Mix ingredients until thin enough to drizzle.

High Altitude (3500 to 6500 feet): Heat oven to 425°. Stir 2 tablespoons all-purpose flour into 2 cups Bisquick mix. Use 2 tablespoons granulated sugar.

Betty's **TIP:** Blueberries and lemon team up to make a great fresh-tasting combination for breakfast or even an afternoon snack. To store, wrap tightly and keep at room temperature up to 4 days or refrigerate up to a week.

1 Serving: Calories 320 (Calories from Fat 70); Fat 8g (Saturated 2g); Cholesterol 35mg; Sodium 670mg; Carbohydrate 59g (Dietary Fiber 2g); Protein 5g • **% Daily Value:** Vitamin A 2%; Vitamin C 4%; Calcium 12%; Iron 8% • **Exchanges:** 2 Starch, 2 Other Carbohydrate, 1 Fat • **Carbohydrate Choices:** 4

kids LOVE

Maple–Sour Cream Pancakes

PREP: 10 MIN; COOK: 12 MIN

About 13 pancakes

2 cups Original Bisquick mix

1/3 cup sour cream

2/3 cup milk

1 tablespoon packed brown sugar

2 tablespoons maple-flavored syrup

2 eggs

1. Heat griddle or skillet over medium-high heat (375°); grease with butter if necessary (or spray with cooking spray before heating).

2. Stir all ingredients until blended. Pour batter by slightly less than 1/4 cupfuls onto hot griddle.

3. Cook until edges of pancakes are dry. Turn; cook until golden. Serve with additional syrup if desired.

High Altitude (3500 to 6500 feet): No changes.

Betty's **TIP:** Here's the pancake with syrup cooked right in. For even more maple flavor, top with additional syrup or with Maple-Berry Sauce (page 37).

1 Pancake: Calories 115 (Calories from Fat 45); Fat 5g (Saturated 2g); Cholesterol 35mg; Sodium 280mg; Carbohydrate 15g (Dietary Fiber 0g); Protein 3g · **% Daily Value:** Vitamin A 2%; Vitamin C 0%; Calcium 6%; Iron 4% · **Exchanges:** 1 Starch, 1 Fat · **Carbohydrate Choices:** 1

Maple–Sour Cream Pancakes

Maple-Topped Oven Pancake

PREP: 15 MIN; BAKE: 35 MIN

9 to 12 servings

1/2 cup packed brown sugar

1/3 cup butter or margarine

1/2 cup maple-flavored syrup

1 1/2 cups Original Bisquick mix

1/4 cup packed brown sugar

1 cup milk

2 eggs

1. Heat oven to 350°. Heat 1/2 cup brown sugar, the butter and maple syrup in 1-quart saucepan over low heat, stirring occasionally, until melted and smooth. Pour into ungreased rectangular pan, 13 × 9 × 2 inches.

2. Beat remaining ingredients in medium bowl, using wire whisk or fork, until blended. Carefully pour over syrup mixture.

3. Bake uncovered 30 to 35 minutes or until top springs back when touched in center. Cut into 3-inch squares; turn each square upside down onto plate. Serve immediately with additional syrup if desired.

High Altitude (3500 to 6500 feet): No changes.

Betty's **TIP:** This easy oven pancake bakes in its own syrup. Make this tasty recipe when you want a break from flipping pancakes.

1 Serving: Calories 295 (Calories from Fat 100); Fat 11g (Saturated 3g); Cholesterol 50mg; Sodium 430mg; Carbohydrate 45g (Dietary Fiber 0g); Protein 4g • **% Daily Value:** Vitamin A 6%; Vitamin C 0%; Calcium 8%; Iron 6% • **Exchanges:** 2 Starch, 1 Other Carbohydrate, 2 Fat • **Carbohydrate Choices:** 3

Dutch Apple Pannekoeken

PREP: 15 MIN; BAKE: 23 MIN

6 servings

1/4 cup packed brown sugar

1/4 teaspoon ground cinnamon

2 medium cooking apples, peeled and thinly sliced (2 cups)

1/3 cup water

2 tablespoons butter or margarine

1/2 cup Original Bisquick mix

2 eggs

1. Heat oven to 400°. Generously grease pie plate, 9 × 1 1/4 inches, with shortening or spray with cooking spray. Mix brown sugar and cinnamon in medium bowl. Add apples; toss and set aside.

2. Heat water and butter to boiling in 2-quart saucepan; reduce heat to low. Add Bisquick mix; stir vigorously until mixture forms a ball; remove from heat. Beat in eggs, one at a time. Continue beating until smooth.

3. Spread batter in bottom of pie plate. Arrange apples on top to within 1 inch of edge of pie plate. Bake about 23 minutes or until puffed and edge is golden brown. Serve immediately.

High Altitude (3500 to 6500 feet): Heat oven to 450°.

Betty's **TIP:** Slightly tart apples with a crisp texture, such as Granny Smith or Haralson, are great ones to use. Sprinkle this puffy pancake with powdered sugar, and serve with warm maple syrup. For Dutch Pear Pannekoeken, use 2 pears, sliced, instead of the apples.

1 Serving: Calories 160 (Calories from Fat 65); Fat 7g (Saturated 3g); Cholesterol 80mg; Sodium 190mg; Carbohydrate 22g (Dietary Fiber 1g); Protein 3g · **% Daily Value:** Vitamin A 4%; Vitamin C 0%; Calcium 4%; Iron 4% · **Exchanges:** 1 Starch, 1/2 Fruit, 1 Fat · **Carbohydrate Choices:** 1 1/2

Baked Pear Pancake

PREP: 15 MIN; BAKE: 25 MIN

8 servings

1/4 cup butter or margarine

1 cup Original or Reduced Fat Bisquick mix

3/4 cup milk

4 eggs

2 medium pears, peeled and thinly sliced

1/4 cup sugar

1/4 teaspoon ground cinnamon

Honey-Raisin Syrup (below)

Honey-Raisin Syrup

1/2 cup honey

1/4 cup butter or margarine

1/4 cup golden raisins

1/4 teaspoon ground cinnamon

1. Heat oven to 400°. Place 2 tablespoons of the butter in each of 2 pie plates, 9 × 1 1/4 inches. Heat in oven until butter melts.

2. Beat Bisquick mix, milk and eggs in small bowl, using wire whisk or fork, until smooth. Arrange half of the pear slices in each pie plate. Divide batter evenly between pie plates. Mix sugar and cinnamon; sprinkle over batter.

3. Bake 20 to 25 minutes or until puffed and golden brown. Make Honey-Raisin Syrup; serve with pancakes.

Honey-Raisin Syrup

Heat all ingredients over medium heat, stirring occasionally, until hot.

High Altitude (3500 to 6500 feet): No changes.

Betty's **TIP:** For a fruity way to start your day, this pear pancake with its raisin syrup is a winner. If you'd rather use peaches, just substitute fresh peaches, or use 1 1/2 cups canned (drained) or frozen (thawed) sliced peaches.

1 Serving: Calories 345 (Calories from Fat 155); Fat 17g (Saturated 8g); Cholesterol 140mg; Sodium 320mg; Carbohydrate 43g (Dietary Fiber 1g); Protein 5g • **% Daily Value:** Vitamin A 12%; Vitamin C 0%; Calcium 8%; Iron 6% • **Exchanges:** 2 Starch, 1 Other Carbohydrate, 3 Fat • **Carbohydrate Choices:** 3

Praline Peach Pancakes

PREP: 10 MIN; COOK: 15 MIN

About 12 pancakes

Praline Peach Syrup (below)

2 cups Original or Reduced Fat
  Bisquick mix

1 cup fat-free (skim) milk

2 tablespoons pecan pieces

1 tablespoon packed brown sugar

1 egg

1 container (6 ounces) peach
  yogurt (2/3 cup)

Praline Peach Syrup

1/2 cup maple-flavored syrup

1/4 cup pecan pieces

1 medium peach or nectarine,
  peeled and chopped (3/4 cup)

1. Make Praline Peach Syrup; keep warm. Heat griddle or skillet over medium-high heat (375°); grease with butter if necessary (or spray with cooking spray before heating).

2. Stir remaining ingredients until blended. Pour batter by slightly less than 1/4 cupfuls onto hot griddle.

3. Cook until edges of pancakes are dry. Turn; cook until golden brown. Serve with syrup.

Praline Peach Syrup

Heat all ingredients in 1-quart saucepan over low heat, stirring occasionally, until hot.

High Altitude (3500 to 6500 feet): No changes.

Betty's **TIP:** Looking for a hot weekday breakfast? You can make these pancakes, stack them between sheets of waxed paper and freeze them in a plastic food-storage bag or container. Then, when desired, pop them into your toaster or toaster oven for piping-hot pancakes in minutes. Make the syrup as the pancakes reheat.

1 Pancake (with 1 tablespoon syrup):
Calories 175 (Calories from Fat 55); Fat 6g (Saturated 1g); Cholesterol 20mg; Sodium 320mg; Carbohydrate 28g (Dietary Fiber 1g); Protein 4g • % **Daily Value:** Vitamin A 2%; Vitamin C 0%; Calcium 8%; Iron 4% • **Exchanges:** 1 Starch, 1 Other Carbohydrate, 1 Fat • **Carbohydrate Choices:** 2

Southwest Corn Pancakes

PREP: 10 MIN; COOK: 12 MIN

About 13 pancakes

1 1/2 cups Original Bisquick mix

1/2 cup cornmeal

1 cup milk

2 eggs

1/2 cup shredded Monterey Jack cheese (2 ounces)

1/2 cup drained canned whole kernel corn

1/4 cup canned chopped green chiles

1 teaspoon chili powder

Sour cream, if desired

Salsa, if desired

Shredded lettuce, if desired

Sliced ripe olives, if desired

1. Heat griddle or skillet over medium-high heat (375°); grease with butter if necessary (or spray with cooking spray before heating).

2. Stir Bisquick mix, cornmeal, milk and eggs in large bowl until blended. Stir in cheese, corn, chiles and chili powder. Pour batter by slightly less than 1/4 cupfuls onto hot griddle; spread slightly.

3. Cook until edges of pancakes are dry. Turn; cook until golden. Serve with sour cream, salsa, lettuce and olives.

High Altitude (3500 to 6500 feet): No changes.

Betty's **TIP:** These savory pancakes make an easy and yummy dinner served with chorizo or another sausage and sliced fresh fruit, such as mango and pineapple.

1 Pancake: Calories 115 (Calories from Fat 45); Fat 5g (Saturated 2g); Cholesterol 40mg; Sodium 300mg; Carbohydrate 15g (Dietary Fiber 1g); Protein 4g • **% Daily Value:** Vitamin A 2%; Vitamin C 0%; Calcium 8%; Iron 4% • **Exchanges:** 1 Starch, 1 Fat • **Carbohydrate Choices:** 1

Southwest Corn Pancakes

P B and J Stacks
PREP: 10 MIN; COOK: 12 MIN

About 18 pancakes

"J" Syrup (below)
2 cups Original Bisquick mix
1/2 cup peanut butter
1 1/2 cups milk
2 eggs

"J" Syrup
1 cup fruit jam, jelly or preserves
1 cup maple-flavored syrup

1. Make "J" Syrup; keep warm. Heat griddle or skillet over medium-high heat (375°); grease with butter if necessary (or spray with cooking spray before heating).

2. Beat remaining ingredients with wire whisk until blended. Pour batter by slightly less than 1/4 cupfuls onto hot griddle.

3. Cook until edges of pancakes are dry. Turn; cook until golden. Serve stacks of pancakes with "J" Syrup and, if desired, additional peanut butter.

"J" Syrup
Heat ingredients in 2-quart saucepan over medium heat, stirring occasionally, until warm.

High Altitude (3500 to 6500 feet): No changes.

Betty's **TIP:** Experiment mixing the syrup with different jams and jellies to find the one your family likes best. For another easy pancake topping, mix equal amounts of plain or vanilla yogurt and any flavor of fruit preserves.

1 Pancake (with about 2 tablespoons syrup): Calories 215 (Calories from Fat 65); Fat 7g (Saturated 2g); Cholesterol 25mg; Sodium 270mg; Carbohydrate 35g (Dietary Fiber 1g); Protein 4g • **% Daily Value:** Vitamin A 2%; Vitamin C 0%; Calcium 6%; Iron 4% • **Exchanges:** 1 1/2 Starch, 1/2 Other Carbohydrate, 1 1/2 Fat • **Carbohydrate Choices:** 2

P B and J Stacks

kids
LOVE

ULTIMATE Melt-in-Your-Mouth Pancakes

PREP: 4 MIN; COOK: 18 MIN

About 14 pancakes

2 cups Original Bisquick mix

1 cup milk

1 tablespoon sugar

2 tablespoons lemon juice

2 teaspoons baking powder

2 eggs

1. Heat griddle or skillet over medium-high heat (375°); grease with butter if necessary (or spray with cooking spray before heating).

2. Stir all ingredients until blended. Pour batter by slightly less than 1/4 cupfuls onto hot griddle.

3. Cook until edges are dry. Turn; cook until golden.

High Altitude (3500 to 6500 feet): No changes.

Betty's **TIP:** Want your favorite Bisquick pancakes jazzed up a little? Here's the recipe that does just that and is still very easy to make. Top with Maple-Berry Sauce (page 37) or Ultimate Syrup (page 33).

1 Pancake: Calories 95 (Calories from Fat 25); Fat 3g (Saturated 1g); Cholesterol 30mg; Sodium 330mg; Carbohydrate 13g (Dietary Fiber 0g); Protein 3g • **% Daily Value:** Vitamin A 2%; Vitamin C 0%; Calcium 8%; Iron 4% • **Exchanges:** 1 Starch, 1/2 Fat • **Carbohydrate Choices:** 1

ULTIMATE Best-Ever Waffles

PREP: 8 MIN; BAKE: 16 MIN

8 servings (two 4-inch waffles each)

Ultimate Syrup (below)

2 cups Original Bisquick mix

1 1/4 cups milk

2 tablespoons sugar

2 tablespoons lemon juice

2 tablespoons melted butter, melted margarine or vegetable oil

1/4 teaspoon baking soda

1 egg

Ultimate Syrup

1/4 cup hazelnut spread with skim milk and cocoa (from 13-ounce jar)

3/4 cup light corn syrup

2 tablespoons water

1. Make Ultimate Syrup; keep warm. Heat waffle iron; grease with vegetable oil if necessary (or spray with cooking spray before heating).

2. Stir remaining ingredients until blended. Pour batter for waffle onto center of hot waffle iron. Close lid of waffle iron.

3. Bake 3 to 4 minutes or until steaming stops. Carefully remove waffle. Repeat with remaining batter. Serve with syrup.

Ultimate Syrup

Stir all ingredients in microwavable pitcher or bowl. Microwave uncovered on High 30 to 45 seconds or until warm.

High Altitude (3500 to 6500 feet): No changes.

Betty's **TIP:** What could be better than the ultimate waffle with the ultimate syrup for breakfast or brunch? If you happen to have leftover waffles, refrigerate them and then reheat in the toaster another day.

1 Serving: Calories 325 (Calories from Fat 100); Fat 11g (Saturated 4g); Cholesterol 35mg; Sodium 600mg; Carbohydrate 51g (Dietary Fiber 1g); Protein 6g • **% Daily Value:** Vitamin A 4%; Vitamin C 0%; Calcium 10%; Iron 6% • **Exchanges:** 2 Starch, 1 1/2 Other Carbohydrate, 2 Fat • **Carbohydrate Choices:** 3 1/2

kids LOVE

Bacon and Swiss Waffles

PREP: 10 MIN; BAKE: 12 MIN

12 servings (one 4-inch waffle square)

2 cups Original or Reduced Fat Bisquick mix

1 1/2 cups milk

2 eggs

1 cup shredded Swiss cheese (4 ounces)

8 slices bacon, crisply cooked and crumbled (1/2 cup)

1. Heat waffle iron; grease with vegetable oil if necessary (or spray with cooking spray before heating). Stir Bisquick mix, milk and eggs in large bowl until blended. Stir in cheese and bacon.

2. Pour batter by slightly less than 1 cupfuls onto center of hot waffle iron.

3. Bake 3 to 4 minutes or until steaming stops and waffle is golden brown. Carefully remove waffle. Repeat with remaining batter.

High Altitude (3500 to 6500 feet): No changes.

Betty's **TIP:** Mix the waffle batter in a 4-cup glass measuring cup that has a handle and spout; the batter will be easy to pour onto the waffle iron. Cheddar or mozzarella cheese can be used instead of the Swiss cheese.

1 Serving: Calories 330 (Calories from Fat 160); Fat 18g (Saturated 8g); Cholesterol 100mg; Sodium 800mg; Carbohydrate 28g (Dietary Fiber 0g); Protein 14g • **% Daily Value:** Vitamin A 8%; Vitamin C 0%; Calcium 32%; Iron 8% • **Exchanges:** 2 Starch, 1 High-Fat Meat, 2 Fat • **Carbohydrate Choices:** 2

Bacon and Swiss Waffles

Glorious Morning Waffles

PREP: 15 MIN; COOK: 15 MIN

6 servings (two 4-inch waffles each)

2 cups Original Bisquick mix

1/2 cup shredded peeled all-purpose apple (1 small)

1/4 cup shredded carrot

1/4 cup chopped nuts, if desired

1 1/3 cups milk

2 tablespoons vegetable oil

1 teaspoon ground cinnamon

1 egg

Maple syrup or honey, if desired

1. Heat waffle iron; grease with vegetable oil if necessary (or spray with cooking spray before heating).

2. Stir all ingredients except syrup until blended. Pour batter by slightly less than 1 cupfuls onto center of hot waffle iron.

3. Bake about 5 minutes or until steaming stops and waffle is golden brown. Carefully remove waffle. Repeat with remaining batter. Serve waffles with syrup.

High Altitude (3500 to 6500 feet): No changes.

Betty's **TIP:** For a fun serving idea kids will like, cut waffles into strips with a pizza cutter and dip into syrup. To store, tightly wrap cooked waffles and freeze; reheat by toasting in your toaster.

1 Waffle: Calories 250 (Calories from Fat 110); Fat 12g (Saturated 3g); Cholesterol 40mg; Sodium 610mg; Carbohydrate 30g (Dietary Fiber 1g); Protein 6g • **% Daily Value:** Vitamin A 20%; Vitamin C 0%; Calcium 14%; Iron 8% • **Exchanges:** 2 Starch, 2 Fat • **Carbohydrate Choices:** 2

Granola-Wheat Waffles with Maple-Berry Sauce

PREP: 10 MIN; BAKE: 18 MIN

12 servings (two 4-inch waffles each)

Maple-Berry Sauce (below)
1 1/2 cups Original Bisquick mix
1/2 cup granola cereal
1/2 cup whole wheat flour
1 1/2 cups milk
3 tablespoons vegetable oil
2 eggs
1 container (6 ounces) strawberry yogurt (2/3 cup)

Maple-Berry Sauce

2/3 cup maple-flavored syrup
1 cup strawberries, cut into fourths

1. Make Maple-Berry Sauce; keep warm. Heat waffle iron; grease with vegetable oil if necessary (or spray with cooking spray before heating).

2. Stir remaining ingredients until blended. Pour batter by 2/3 cupfuls onto center of hot waffle iron.

3. Bake 2 to 3 minutes or until steaming stops and waffle is golden brown. Carefully remove waffle. Repeat with remaining batter. Serve waffles with sauce.

Maple-Berry Sauce
Heat maple syrup to boiling in 1 1/2-quart saucepan, stirring occasionally. Stir in strawberries; remove from heat.

High Altitude (3500 to 6500 feet): Bake about 4 minutes.

Betty's **TIP:** You can use almost any flavor of yogurt in these waffles—raspberry, vanilla and strawberry-banana are great choices. If you prefer, skip the Maple-Berry Sauce, and top these waffles with a dollop of yogurt and a sprinkle of additional granola.

1 Serving: Calories 135 (Calories from Fat 35); Fat 4g (Saturated 2g); Cholesterol 20mg; Sodium 140mg; Carbohydrate 23g (Dietary Fiber 1g); Protein 2g • **% Daily Value:** Vitamin A 0%; Vitamin C 4%; Calcium 4%; Iron 2% • **Exchanges:** 1 Starch, 1/2 Other Carbohydrate, 1/2 Fat • **Carbohydrate Choices:** 1 1/2

Tiramisu Waffles

PREP: 10 MIN; COOK: 15 MIN

12 servings (one 4-inch waffle each)

Tiramisu Topping (below)

1 1/2 cups Original Bisquick mix

1 cup sugar

1/3 cup baking cocoa

3/4 cup water

2 tablespoons vegetable oil

2 eggs

1 cup hot strong coffee

Tiramisu Topping

1 package (8 ounces) cream cheese, softened

1/2 cup sugar

1/2 cup chocolate-flavored syrup

1 container (8 ounces) frozen whipped topping, thawed

1. Make Tiramisu Topping; refrigerate while making waffles. Heat waffle iron; grease with vegetable oil if necessary (or spray with cooking spray before heating).

2. Stir remaining ingredients except coffee until blended. Pour batter by slightly less than 1 cupfuls onto center of hot waffle iron.

3. Bake about 5 minutes or until steaming stops. Carefully remove waffle. Repeat with remaining batter. Drizzle coffee over waffles. Spoon topping onto waffles. Sprinkle with additional baking cocoa if desired.

Tiramisu Topping
Beat cream cheese, sugar and chocolate syrup in large bowl with electric mixer on medium speed until smooth. Gently stir in whipped topping until blended.

High Altitude (3500 to 6500 feet): Use 3/4 cup sugar in waffles and add 1/4 cup all-purpose flour.

Betty's **TIP:** For coffee and cocoa lovers, this waffle is a tasty rendition of the popular dessert. Because waffle irons come in a variety of shapes and sizes, which use varying amounts of batter, you may end up with a few less or a few more waffles.

1 Serving: Calories 350 (Calories from Fat 145); Fat 16g (Saturated 8g); Cholesterol 70mg; Sodium 310mg; Carbohydrate 47g (Dietary Fiber 1g); Protein 5g • **% Daily Value:** Vitamin A 10%; Vitamin C 0%; Calcium 6%; Iron 8% • **Exchanges:** 1 1/2 Starch, 1 1/2 Other Carbohydrate, 3 Fat • **Carbohydrate Choices:** 3

Tiramisu Waffles

Cinnamon Batter-Dipped French Toast

kids LOVE

PREP: 10 MIN; COOK: 12 MIN

10 slices

2 cups Original Bisquick mix

1 1/4 cups milk

2 teaspoons ground cinnamon

1 teaspoon vanilla

2 eggs

10 slices bread

Powdered sugar, if desired

Maple syrup, if desired

1. Heat griddle or skillet over medium-high heat (375°); grease with butter if necessary (or spray with cooking spray before heating).

2. Stir Bisquick mix, milk, cinnamon, vanilla and eggs until blended. Dip bread into batter; drain excess batter back into bowl. Place on hot griddle.

3. Cook 1 to 2 minutes on each side or until golden brown. Sprinkle with powdered sugar; serve with syrup.

High Altitude (3500 to 6500 feet): No changes.

Betty's **TIP:** Use any leftover bread to make this old-fashioned French toast. French and Italian breads work well, and they have a round shape that fits nicely in a skillet or griddle.

1 Slice: Calories 195 (Calories from Fat 55); Fat 6g (Saturated 2g); Cholesterol 45mg; Sodium 500mg; Carbohydrate 29g (Dietary Fiber 1g); Protein 6g • **% Daily Value:** Vitamin A 2%; Vitamin C 0%; Calcium 12%; Iron 10% • **Exchanges:** 2 Starch, 1 Fat • **Carbohydrate Choices:** 2

Turkey Sausage Quiche

PREP: 15 MIN; BAKE: 35 MIN; STAND: 10 MIN

6 servings

1 1/4 cups Original Bisquick mix

1/4 cup butter or margarine, softened

2 tablespoons boiling water

1 cup shredded Italian-style cheese blend (4 ounces)

1 cup cooked turkey sausage

4 medium green onions, sliced (1/4 cup)

1 1/2 cups half-and-half

3 eggs

1 teaspoon chopped fresh basil leaves

1. Heat oven to 400°. Spray pie plate, 9 × 1 1/4 inches, with cooking spray. Stir Bisquick mix and butter until blended. Add boiling water; stir vigorously until soft dough forms. Press dough on bottom and up side of pie plate, forming edge on rim of pie plate.

2. Sprinkle cheese, sausage and onions over crust. Beat half-and-half and eggs with wire whisk until blended; stir in basil. Pour into crust.

3. Bake 30 to 35 minutes or until knife inserted in center comes out clean. Let stand 10 minutes before cutting.

High Altitude (3500 to 6500 feet): Use 2 tablespoons butter. Bake 38 to 42 minutes.

Betty's **TIP:** Cooked Italian sausage can be substituted for the turkey sausage. Or, for another tasty variation, try Canadian Bacon and Cheese Quiche: Use 1 cup chopped Canadian-style bacon and 1 cup shredded Swiss cheese in place of the turkey sausage and Italian-style cheese blend; substitute parsley for the basil.

1 Serving: Calories 390 (Calories from Fat 245); Fat 27g (Saturated 14g); Cholesterol 170mg; Sodium 700mg; Carbohydrate 20g (Dietary Fiber 1g); Protein 16g • % **Daily Value:** Vitamin A 18%; Vitamin C 4%; Calcium 26%; Iron 8% • **Exchanges:** 1 Starch, 2 High-Fat Meat, 1 1/2 Fat • **Carbohydrate Choices:** 1

Peanut Butter Waffle Toast

PREP: 5 MIN; BAKE: 15 MIN

6 to 8 servings

1 1/4 cups milk

1 cup Original Bisquick mix

1/2 cup peanut butter

2 tablespoons granulated sugar

1 teaspoon vanilla

1 egg

6 to 8 slices bread

6 to 8 tablespoons miniature semisweet chocolate chips

Powdered sugar, if desired

1. Heat waffle iron; grease with vegetable oil if necessary (or spray with cooking spray before heating).

2. Stir milk, Bisquick mix, peanut butter, granulated sugar, vanilla and egg until well blended. Carefully dip bread into batter on both sides. (If coating seems too thick, add milk, 1 teaspoon at a time, until desired consistency is reached.) Place in waffle iron; close lid.

3. Bake about 2 minutes or until steaming stops and "toast" is golden. Carefully remove waffle toast. Sprinkle each waffle toast with 1 tablespoon chocolate chips and powdered sugar.

High Altitude (3500 to 6500 feet): Bake about 3 minutes.

Betty's **TIP:** Dipping the bread in a peanut butter batter and cooking it in a waffle iron makes this recipe a cross between French toast and a waffle. When coating the bread with the thick batter, turning it with a fork or spatula is a less messy way to get the job done.

1 Serving: Calories 395 (Calories from Fat 180); Fat 20g (Saturated 6g); Cholesterol 40mg; Sodium 560mg; Carbohydrate 42g (Dietary Fiber 3g); Protein 12g • **% Daily Value:** Vitamin A 2%; Vitamin C 0%; Calcium 14%; Iron 12% • **Exchanges:** 3 Starch, 1/2 High-Fat Meat, 2 1/2 Fat • **Carbohydrate Choices:** 3

Peanut Butter Waffle Toast

Baked Turkey, Cheddar and Bacon Sandwich

PREP: 10 MIN; BAKE: 32 MIN; STAND: 5 MIN

6 servings

2 cups Original Bisquick mix

1 cup milk

1 egg

4 ounces thinly sliced deli turkey breast

1 1/2 cups shredded Cheddar cheese (6 ounces)

5 slices cooked bacon

1. Heat oven to 400°. Spray square baking dish, 8 × 8 × 2 inches, with cooking spray.

2. Stir Bisquick mix, milk and egg until blended. Spread half of the batter in baking dish. Top with turkey, 1 cup of the cheese and the bacon. Spread remaining batter over bacon.

3. Bake uncovered about 29 minutes or until golden brown and center is set. Sprinkle with remaining 1/2 cup cheese. Bake about 3 minutes or until cheese is melted. Let stand 5 minutes before cutting.

High Altitude (3500 to 6500 feet): Increase first bake time to about 32 minutes.

Betty's **TIP:** This hot sandwich has all the delicious flavors of a club sandwich in a convenient, totable package. Wrap each serving in a sheet of aluminum foil, and bring some fresh fruit and cookies for a hot portable meal.

1 Serving: Calories 355 (Calories from Fat 180); Fat 20g (Saturated 9g); Cholesterol 80mg; Sodium 1080mg; Carbohydrate 27g (Dietary Fiber 0g); Protein 17g • **% Daily Value:** Vitamin A 8%; Vitamin C 0%; Calcium 26%; Iron 10% • **Exchanges:** 2 Starch, 1 1/2 Medium-Fat Meat, 2 Fat • **Carbohydrate Choices:** 2

Baked Turkey, Cheddar and Bacon Sandwich

Roasted-Vegetable Egg Bake

PREP: 15 MIN; BAKE: 30 MIN

8 servings

1 tablespoon olive or vegetable oil

1 large onion, chopped (1 cup)

1 bag (26 ounces) frozen Parmesan herb-flavor oven-roasted potatoes, vegetables and cheese seasoning meal starter

1 cup Original Bisquick mix

1 1/2 cups milk

4 eggs

1 cup shredded Italian-style cheese blend or mozzarella cheese (4 ounces)

1. Heat oven to 400°. Spray rectangular baking dish, 13 × 9 × 2 inches, with cooking spray. Heat oil in 12-inch nonstick skillet over medium heat. Cook onion and frozen vegetables in oil 8 to 10 minutes, stirring occasionally, until vegetables are heated through and crisp-tender. Sprinkle vegetables with contents of seasoning packet from vegetables; stir gently to coat. Spread in baking dish.

2. Stir Bisquick mix, milk and eggs until blended. Pour over vegetables in baking dish.

3. Bake uncovered about 25 minutes or until knife inserted in center comes out clean. Sprinkle with cheese. Bake about 5 minutes or until cheese is melted.

High Altitude (3500 to 6500 feet): No changes.

Betty's **TIP:** Other meal starter vegetable blends are available with different vegetable combinations and seasonings. Any of them can be used in this recipe. If you'd like, add 1 cup chopped cooked chicken or turkey with the seasoning packet from the vegetables.

1 Serving: Calories 280 (Calories from Fat 115); Fat 13g (Saturated 6g); Cholesterol 130mg; Sodium 980mg; Carbohydrate 27g (Dietary Fiber 2g); Protein 14g • **% Daily Value:** Vitamin A 22%; Vitamin C 8%; Calcium 24%; Iron 8% • **Exchanges:** 2 Starch, 1 Medium-Fat Meat, 1 Fat • **Carbohydrate Choices:** 2

Roasted-Vegetable Egg Bake

Ham and Asparagus Breakfast Bake

PREP: 15 MIN; BAKE: 30 MIN

6 servings

2 cups 1-inch pieces asparagus

1 1/2 cups diced fully cooked ham

1/2 cup milk

1 can (10 3/4 ounces) condensed cream of asparagus soup

1 cup shredded Italian-style cheese blend (4 ounces)

1 cup Original Bisquick mix

3/4 cup milk

1. Heat oven to 400°. Heat asparagus, ham, milk, soup and 3/4 cup of the cheese to boiling in 3-quart saucepan, stirring constantly. Boil and stir 1 minute. Spread in ungreased 2-quart casserole.

2. Stir Bisquick mix, milk and remaining 1/4 cup cheese until blended. Pour evenly over ham mixture.

3. Bake uncovered about 30 minutes or until golden brown and toothpick inserted in biscuit layer comes out clean.

High Altitude (3500 to 6500 feet): Bake about 35 minutes.

Betty's **TIP:** A 9-ounce package of frozen asparagus cuts, thawed and drained, can be used as a substitute for the fresh. If you can't find cream of asparagus soup, try cream of chicken or cream of celery. For variety, look for different types of cheeses, such as six-cheese, roasted garlic and other flavors—all work well in this dish.

1 Serving: Calories 290 (Calories from Fat 135); Fat 15g (Saturated 6g); Cholesterol 40mg; Sodium 1290mg; Carbohydrate 21g (Dietary Fiber 1g); Protein 18g • **% Daily Value:** Vitamin A 16%; Vitamin C 12%; Calcium 24%; Iron 10% • **Exchanges:** 1 Starch, 1 Vegetable, 1 High-Fat Meat, 2 Fat • **Carbohydrate Choices:** 1 1/2

Garden Vegetable Bake

PREP: 15 MIN; BAKE: 35 MIN; STAND: 5 MIN

6 servings

1/2 cup grated reduced-fat Parmesan cheese topping

1 cup chopped zucchini

2/3 cup drained canned whole kernel corn

1 small tomato, chopped (1/2 cup)

1 medium onion, chopped (1/2 cup)

3/4 cup Original or Reduced Fat Bisquick mix

1 cup fat-free (skim) milk

2 eggs, 1/2 cup fat-free cholesterol-free egg product or 4 egg whites

1/2 teaspoon salt

1/4 teaspoon pepper

1. Heat oven to 400°. Spray square baking dish, $8 \times 8 \times 2$ inches, with cooking spray. Sprinkle 1/4 cup of the cheese in baking dish. Top with zucchini, corn, tomato and onion. Sprinkle remaining 1/4 cup cheese over vegetables.

2. Stir remaining ingredients until blended. Pour over vegetables and cheese.

3. Bake uncovered 32 to 35 minutes or until knife inserted in center comes out clean. Let stand 5 minutes before cutting.

High Altitude (3500 to 6500 feet): Use 1 cup Bisquick mix. Bake 35 to 38 minutes.

Betty's **TIP:** A summer garden or farmers' market is a great place to look for the zucchini. Or instead of the zucchini, use 1 cup green peas, chopped broccoli or 1-inch asparagus pieces. For Chicken Garden Bake, add two 5-ounce cans of chunk chicken, drained, or 1 cup cut-up cooked chicken with the vegetables.

1 Serving: Calories 145 (Calories from Fat 20); Fat 2g (Saturated 1g); Cholesterol 5mg; Sodium 560mg; Carbohydrate 25g (Dietary Fiber 3g); Protein 7g • **% Daily Value:** Vitamin A 10%; Vitamin C 6%; Calcium 10%; Iron 6% • **Exchanges:** 1 Starch, 1 Vegetable, 1/2 Fat • **Carbohydrate Choices:** 1 1/2

Chapter 2

SIMPLE
SNACKS and

Cheddar–Green Olive Breadsticks (page 65), Savory Cheese Triangles (page 64) and Far East Canapés (page 58)

Breads

Turkey Mini-Sandwiches

PREP: 10 MIN; BAKE: 50 MIN; STAND: 5 MIN

18 mini-sandwiches

2 cups Original Bisquick mix

1/2 cup dried cranberries

1 cup milk

2 tablespoons yellow mustard

1 egg

1 package (6 ounces) thinly sliced fully cooked smoked turkey, chopped

1 cup shredded Swiss cheese (4 ounces)

1. Heat oven to 350°. Spray bottom and sides of square baking dish, 8 × 8 × 2 inches, with cooking spray.

2. Stir Bisquick mix, cranberries, milk, mustard and egg until blended. Pour half of the batter into baking dish. Top with half of the turkey; sprinkle with 1/2 cup of the cheese to within 1/4 inch of edges of baking dish. Top with remaining turkey. Pour remaining batter over turkey.

3. Bake uncovered 45 to 50 minutes or until golden brown and set. Sprinkle with remaining 1/2 cup cheese. Let stand 5 minutes before cutting. Cut into 9 squares; cut each square diagonally in half.

High Altitude (3500 to 6500 feet): Bake 47 to 52 minutes.

Betty's **TIP:** Make it easier on yourself! Bake these sandwiches the day before and cut into serving pieces. Store covered in the refrigerator, and serve cold the next day. Or, to serve warm, place serving pieces on a cookie sheet, cover loosely with aluminum foil and reheat in 350° oven about 10 minutes or until warm.

1 Mini-Sandwich: Calories 115 (Calories from Fat 45); Fat 5g (Saturated 2g); Cholesterol 25mg; Sodium 350mg; Carbohydrate 12g (Dietary Fiber 0g); Protein 5g • **% Daily Value:** Vitamin A 2%; Vitamin C 0%; Calcium 10%; Iron 2% • **Exchanges:** 1 Starch, 1 Fat • **Carbohydrate Choices:** 1

Turkey Mini-Sandwiches

Quick Chicken Chunks

PREP: 10 MIN; MICROWAVE: 8 MIN

6 servings

1 1/2 cups cornflakes cereal

1/2 cup Original Bisquick mix

3/4 teaspoon paprika

1/4 teaspoon salt

1/4 teaspoon pepper

1 pound boneless, skinless chicken breasts, cut into 1-inch pieces

1 tablespoon vegetable oil

1. Place cereal in 2-quart resealable plastic food-storage bag; crush with rolling pin. Add Bisquick mix, paprika, salt and pepper to cereal in plastic bag; shake gently to mix.

2. In medium bowl mix chicken and oil. Shake about 6 chicken pieces at a time in bag until coated with cereal mixture. Shake off any extra crumbs. Place chicken pieces in single layer on waxed paper on microwavable plate. Cover with another sheet of waxed paper.

3. Microwave on High 3 minutes. Turn plate 1/2 turn. Microwave 4 to 5 minutes longer or until chicken is no longer pink in center.

High Altitude (3500 to 6500 feet): No changes.

Betty's **TIP:** You may find that using kitchen scissors makes cutting the chicken easier. Dip these tender chicken chunks into barbecue sauce or honey mustard; you can make your own by mixing equal amounts of honey with your favorite mustard.

1 Serving: Calories 165 (Calories from Fat 55); Fat 6g (Saturated 1g); Cholesterol 45mg; Sodium 360mg; Carbohydrate 12g (Dietary Fiber 0g); Protein 18g • **% Daily Value:** Vitamin A 4%; Vitamin C 2%; Calcium 2%; Iron 16% • **Exchanges:** 1 Starch, 2 Very Lean Meat • **Carbohydrate Choices:** 1

Shrimp Tarts

PREP: 8 MIN; BAKE: 20 MIN; COOL: 5 MIN

24 tarts

1/2 cup Original Bisquick mix

1/2 cup milk

1/4 cup sour cream

1/2 teaspoon Worcestershire
  sauce

2 eggs

2/3 cup shredded Parmesan
  cheese

1/2 cup chopped cooked shrimp

4 medium green onions, sliced
  (1/4 cup)

1. Heat oven to 400°. Spray 24 small muffin cups, 1 3/4 × 1 inch, with cooking spray.

2. Beat Bisquick, milk, sour cream, Worcestershire sauce and eggs in small bowl with spoon until blended. Stir in remaining ingredients. Spoon about 1 tablespoon mixture into each muffin cup.

3. Bake 15 to 20 minutes or until golden. Cool 5 minutes. Loosen sides of tarts from pan; remove from pan.

High Altitude (3500 to 6500 feet): No changes.

Betty's **TIP:** To make tarts one day ahead, remove from muffin pan and place on wire rack to cool, then store tightly covered in the refrigerator. Before serving, place on cookie sheet and cover loosely with aluminum foil. Reheat in 375° oven about 10 minutes or until hot.

1 Tart: Calories 40 (Calories from Fat 20); Fat 2g (Saturated 1g); Cholesterol 30mg; Sodium 110mg; Carbohydrate 2g (Dietary Fiber 0g); Protein 3g • % **Daily Value:** Vitamin A 2%; Vitamin C 0%; Calcium 6%; Iron 3% • **Exchanges:** 1/2 Medium-Fat Meat • **Carbohydrate Choices:** 0

Crab Mini-Quiches

PREP: 15 MIN; BAKE: 20 MIN

24 mini-quiches

1 1/4 cups Original Bisquick mix

1/4 cup butter or margarine, softened

2 tablespoons boiling water

1/3 cup canned crabmeat, finely chopped cooked crabmeat or finely chopped imitation crabmeat

1/2 cup half-and-half

1 egg

2 medium green onions, thinly sliced (2 tablespoons)

1/4 teaspoon salt

1/4 teaspoon ground red pepper (cayenne)

1/2 cup shredded Parmesan cheese

1. Heat oven to 375°. Spray 24 small muffin cups, 1 3/4 × 1 inch, with cooking spray. Stir Bisquick mix and butter in small bowl until blended. Add boiling water; stir vigorously until soft dough forms. Press rounded teaspoonful of dough on bottom and up side of each muffin cup. Divide crabmeat evenly among muffin cups.

2. Beat half-and-half and egg in small bowl with spoon until blended. Stir in onions, salt and red pepper. Spoon 1 1/2 teaspoons egg mixture into each muffin cup. Sprinkle cheese over tops.

3. Bake about 20 minutes or until edges are golden brown and centers are set. Cool 5 minutes. Loosen sides of quiches from pan; remove from pan.

High Altitude (3500 to 6500 feet): No changes.

Betty's **TIP:** These bite-size quiches are great-tasting appetizers. To make one day ahead, remove quiches from muffin pan and place on wire rack to cool, then store tightly covered in the refrigerator. To serve, place on cookie sheet and cover loosely with aluminum foil. Reheat in 375° oven about 10 minutes or until hot.

1 Mini-Quiche: Calories 60 (Calories from Fat 35); Fat 4g (Saturated 2g); Cholesterol 20mg; Sodium 150mg; Carbohydrate 4g (Dietary Fiber 0g); Protein 2g • **% Daily Value:** Vitamin A 2%; Vitamin C 0%; Calcium 4%; Iron 2% • **Exchanges:** 1 Fat • **Carbohydrate Choices:** 0

Crab Mini-Quiches

Far East Canapés

PREP: 15 MIN; BAKE: 17 MIN

Photo on page 51

16 canapés

1 cup Original Bisquick mix

1/4 cup water

1/2 cup finely chopped shaved
turkey (3 ounces)

1/2 cup finely chopped shaved
honey ham (3 ounces)

1/3 cup chutney

3 to 4 tablespoons whipping
(heavy) cream

1/2 teaspoon curry powder

1/4 cup finely shredded Parmesan
cheese

1/4 cup chopped dry-roasted
peanuts

Sliced green onions or fresh
chives, if desired

1. Heat oven to 425°. Spray bottom and sides of square pan, 8 × 8 × 2 inches, with cooking spray.

2. Stir Bisquick mix and water until soft dough forms; beat vigorously with spoon 20 seconds. Pat dough in pan, using fingers dipped in Bisquick mix. Bake 6 to 8 minutes or until crust begins to brown around edges.

3. Mix remaining ingredients except cheese, peanuts and green onions. Spread mixture over baked crust. Sprinkle with cheese. Bake 7 to 9 minutes or until cheese is melted. For canapés, cut into 4 rows by 4 rows. Sprinkle with peanuts; garnish with green onions. Serve warm.

High Altitude (3500 to 6500 feet): Bake crust 7 to 9 minutes. Bake canapés 8 to 10 minutes.

Betty's **TIP:** Keep things simple by buying shaved turkey and ham from the deli when you want to whip up these super-easy appetizers. The chutney, curry and peanuts team up to give you the exotic flavors of Asia in one small bite.

1 Appetizer: Calories 80 (Calories from Fat 35); Fat 4g (Saturated 2g); Cholesterol 10mg; Sodium 270mg; Carbohydrate 7g (Dietary Fiber 0g); Protein 4g • % **Daily Value:** Vitamin A 0%; Vitamin C 0%; Calcium 4%; Iron 2% • **Exchanges:** 1/2 Starch, 1/2 Very Lean Meat, 1/2 Fat • **Carbohydrate Choices:** 1/2

Ranch Veggie Bites

PREP: 15 MIN; COOK: 2 MIN PER BATCH

6 servings

Vegetable oil

3/4 cup Original Bisquick mix

1 teaspoon paprika

1 envelope (1 ounce) ranch
dressing mix

1 tablespoon water

1 egg, slightly beaten

4 cups 1 1/2-inch pieces assorted
vegetables, such as onion
wedges, bell pepper strips,
broccoli flowerets or mushrooms

Sour cream, if desired

1. Pour oil into 3-quart saucepan until 1 inch deep. Heat over medium-high heat to 375°.

2. Mix Bisquick mix, paprika and dressing mix (dry) in resealable plastic food-storage bag. Mix water and egg in large bowl. Add vegetables to egg mixture; stir well to coat. Transfer vegetables to plastic bag with slotted spoon. Seal bag and shake to coat with Bisquick mixture.

3. Fry batches of vegetables in oil 1 to 2 minutes or until light golden brown. Remove from oil with slotted spoon; drain on paper towels. Serve immediately with sour cream.

High Altitude (3500 to 6500 feet): Heat oil to 350° to 365°.

Betty's **TIP:** These battered, deep-fried bites will convince even the most reluctant kids to eat their veggies! Dip them into reduced-fat ranch or Caesar dressing instead of sour cream for a little flavor variation.

1 Serving: Calories 305 (Calories from Fat 25); Fat 25g (Saturated 4g); Cholesterol 35mg; Sodium 570mg; Carbohydrate 16g (Dietary Fiber 1g); Protein 4g · **% Daily Value:** Vitamin A 10%; Vitamin C 22%; Calcium 6%; Iron 6% · **Exchanges:** 1/2 Starch, 1 1/2 Vegetable, 5 Fat · **Carbohydrate Choices:** 1

kids LOVE

Mini White Pizzas

PREP: 13 MIN; BAKE: 11 MIN

4 servings

1 1/2 cups Original Bisquick mix

1/3 cup boiling water

1/2 cup reduced-fat or regular Alfredo sauce

1/2 cup finely chopped cooked chicken

1/2 cup chopped fresh mushrooms

2 tablespoons chopped fresh or 1 teaspoon dried basil leaves

1 cup shredded mozzarella cheese (4 ounces)

Additional fresh basil leaves, if desired

1. Heat oven to 450°. Spray large cookie sheet with cooking spray. Stir Bisquick mix and water until soft dough forms. Divide dough into fourths. Pat each part of dough into 6-inch circle on cookie sheet, using fingers dusted with Bisquick mix; pinch edge to form 1/2-inch rim.

2. Spread Alfredo sauce on dough. Top with chicken, mushrooms and chopped basil. Sprinkle with cheese.

3. Bake 9 to 11 minutes or until crusts are golden brown and cheese is bubbly. Garnish with additional basil leaves.

High Altitude (3500 to 6500 feet): Bake 10 to 12 minutes.

Betty's **TIP:** Using boiling water makes the pizza dough more chewy and flavorful. Keep it to one step by measuring 1/3 cup water in a small glass measuring cup and microwaving on High until full bubbles appear.

1 Pizza: Calories 340 (Calories from Fat 145); Fat 16g (Saturated 7g); Cholesterol 40mg; Sodium 940mg; Carbohydrate 31g (Dietary Fiber 1g); Protein 18g • **% Daily Value:** Vitamin A 8%; Vitamin C 0%; Calcium 34%; Iron 10% • **Exchanges:** 2 Starch, 2 Medium-Fat Meat, 1 Fat • **Carbohydrate Choices:** 2

Mini White Pizzas

kids LOVE

Canadian Bacon–Pineapple Pinwheels

PREP: 15 MIN; BAKE: 18 MIN

12 pinwheels

2 cups Original Bisquick mix

1/2 cup milk

1 can (8 ounces) crushed pineapple, well drained

1 package (3.5 ounces) Canadian-style bacon, chopped

3/4 cup shredded mozzarella cheese (3 ounces)

2 tablespoons butter or margarine, melted

1/4 teaspoon garlic powder

1 cup spaghetti sauce, heated

1. Heat oven to 375°. Spray cookie sheet with cooking spray. Stir Bisquick mix and milk until soft dough forms. Place dough on surface generously dusted with Bisquick mix; gently roll in Bisquick mix to coat. Shape into a ball; knead 10 times.

2. Roll dough into 15 × 10-inch rectangle. Layer pineapple, bacon and cheese on rectangle to within 1 inch of edges. Fold in each 10-inch side of rectangle 1 inch. Beginning at 15-inch side, tightly roll up rectangle; pinch edge into roll to seal. Cut into 12 slices. Place on cookie sheet.

3. Bake 16 to 18 minutes or until light golden and cheese is melted. Mix butter and garlic powder; brush over warm pinwheels. Serve with spaghetti sauce.

High Altitude (3500 to 6500 feet): Bake 17 to 20 minutes.

Betty's **TIP:** Dipped in spaghetti sauce, these yummy little pinwheels have all the flavors of pizza. If your family loves pepperoni, you can substitute 1 package (3.5 ounces) sliced pepperoni for the Canadian bacon.

1 Appetizer: Calories 165 (Calories from Fat 65); Fat 7g (Saturated 3g); Cholesterol 15mg; Sodium 550mg; Carbohydrate 20g (Dietary Fiber 1g); Protein 6g • **% Daily Value:** Vitamin A 6%; Vitamin C 4%; Calcium 10%; Iron 4% • **Exchanges:** 1 Starch, 1/2 Medium-Fat Meat, 1 Fat • **Carbohydrate Choices:** 1

Canadian Bacon–Pineapple Pinwheels

Savory Cheese Triangles

PREP: 15 MIN; BAKE: 13 MIN

Photo on page 50

16 triangles

2 tablespoons firm butter or margarine

1 package (3 ounces) cream cheese

2 cups Original Bisquick mix

1/3 cup milk

1 egg yolk

1/2 cup chive-and-onion cream cheese spread, softened

1/2 cup shredded Gouda cheese (2 ounces)

1 egg white

1 tablespoon chopped fresh parsley, if desired

1. Heat oven to 425°. Cut butter and 3-ounce package of cream cheese into Bisquick mix in medium bowl, using pastry blender or crisscrossing 2 knives, until mixture looks like fine crumbs. Stir in milk and egg yolk. Place dough on surface well dusted with Bisquick mix; gently roll in Bisquick mix to coat. Shape into a ball; knead 10 times.

2. Roll dough into 16 × 8-inch rectangle. Spread chive-and-onion cream cheese lengthwise over half of dough to within 1/4 inch of edges; sprinkle with Gouda cheese. Carefully fold dough over filling. Brush egg white over top; sprinkle with parsley. Cut into four 4-inch squares; cut squares diagonally in half to form 8 triangles. Place on ungreased cookie sheet.

3. Bake 10 to 13 minutes or until golden brown. Cut each triangle in half. Serve warm.

High Altitude (3500 to 6500 feet): No changes.

Betty's **TIP:** Store leftovers tightly covered in the refrigerator. These tasty little gems can be easily reheated in the microwave on High for about 20 to 30 seconds each.

1 Appetizer: Calories 135 (Calories from Fat 80); Fat 9g (Saturated 5g); Cholesterol 35mg; Sodium 300mg; Carbohydrate 10g (Dietary Fiber 0g); Protein 3g • **% Daily Value:** Vitamin A 6%; Vitamin C 0%; Calcium 6%; Iron 4% • **Exchanges:** 1/2 Starch, 2 Fat • **Carbohydrate Choices:** 1/2

kids LOVE

Cheddar–Green Olive Breadsticks

PREP: 15 MIN; BAKE: 14 MIN

Photo on page 50

15 breadsticks

2 1/4 cups Original Bisquick mix

2/3 cup milk

1/2 cup shredded Cheddar cheese
  (2 ounces)

1/3 cup chopped pimiento-stuffed
  green olives

1 egg, beaten

Olive oil or marinara sauce,
  if desired

1. Heat oven to 350°. Spray 2 cookie sheets with cooking spray. Stir Bisquick mix, milk, cheese and olives until soft dough forms. Place dough on surface dusted with Bisquick mix; gently roll in Bisquick mix to coat. Shape into a ball; knead 10 times.

2. Divide dough into 15 equal parts. Roll each into a breadstick about 8 inches long. Place on cookie sheet.

3. Brush egg over dough. Bake 11 to 14 minutes or until light golden brown. Serve warm with olive oil or marinara sauce for dipping.

High Altitude (3500 to 6500 feet): No changes.

Betty's **TIP:** If your family likes green olives, these tasty breads will be a hit at your house. They're great with any soup or salad or as a fun snack. Instead of using olive oil, you can dip them into Creamy Salsa Dip, page 66.

1 Breadstick: Calories 105 (Calories from Fat 45); Fat 5g (Saturated 2g); Cholesterol 15mg; Sodium 370mg; Carbohydrate 12g (Dietary Fiber 0g); Protein 3g • **% Daily Value:** Vitamin A 2%; Vitamin C 0%; Calcium 6%; Iron 4% • **Exchanges:** 1 Starch, 1/2 Fat • **Carbohydrate Choices:** 1

Chili Flatbread with Creamy Salsa Dip

PREP: 7 MIN; BAKE: 10 MIN

24 appetizers

2 cups Original Bisquick mix

1/2 cup hot water

1 tablespoon chili powder

1/2 cup shredded taco-seasoned cheese (2 ounces)

1/4 cup sliced ripe olives

Creamy Salsa Dip (below)

Creamy Salsa Dip

1/2 cup salsa

1/2 cup sour cream

1. Heat oven to 450°. Stir Bisquick mix, water and chili powder until stiff dough forms. Let stand 5 minutes. Place dough on surface sprinkled with Bisquick mix; gently roll in Bisquick mix to coat. Shape into a ball; knead 50 times.

2. Pat or roll dough into 12-inch circle on ungreased cookie sheet. Sprinkle with cheese and olives.

3. Bake 8 to 10 minutes or until edge and cheese are golden brown. Cut in half; cut each half into 12 wedges. Serve warm with Creamy Salsa Dip.

Creamy Salsa Dip
Mix ingredients.

High Altitude (3500 to 6500 feet): No changes.

Betty's **TIP:** Bake and take this simply easy flatbread and dip to your next potluck or party. To tote, place flatbread wedges on a pizza pan, and cover with plastic wrap. Place dip in a covered container.

1 Appetizer: Calories 45 (Calories from Fat 25); Fat 3g (Saturated 1g); Cholesterol 5mg; Sodium 125mg; Carbohydrate 4g (Dietary Fiber 0g); Protein 1g • **% Daily Value:** Vitamin A 4%; Vitamin C 0%; Calcium 2%; Iron 2% • **Exchanges:** 1 Fat • **Carbohydrate Choices:** 0

Chili Flatbread with Creamy Salsa Dip

ULTIMATE Whipped Cream Biscuits

PREP: 8 MIN; BAKE: 12 MIN

12 biscuits

2 cups Original Bisquick mix

2/3 cup whipping (heavy) cream

1. Heat oven to 450°. Stir Bisquick mix and whipping cream until soft dough forms. Place dough on surface well dusted with Bisquick mix; gently roll in Bisquick mix to coat. Shape into a ball; knead 10 times.

2. Roll or pat dough 1/2 inch thick. Cut with 2-inch cutter dipped in Bisquick mix. Place about 1 inch apart on ungreased cookie sheet.

3. Bake 10 to 12 minutes or until golden brown. Serve warm.

High Altitude (3500 to 6500 feet): Heat oven to 425°. Use 1/3 cup cream and 1/3 cup water. Bake 12 to 13 minutes.

Betty's **TIP:** Want great biscuits to serve to company? Look no further— guests would never guess these were made from a mix! To make these tasty breads ahead of time, prepare through step 2, then cover and refrigerate up to 4 hours before baking.

1 Biscuit: Calories 125 (Calories from Fat 65); Fat 7g (Saturated 3g); Cholesterol 15mg; Sodium 290mg; Carbohydrate 13g (Dietary Fiber 0g); Protein 2g • **% Daily Value:** Vitamin A 2%; Vitamin C 0%; Calcium 4%; Iron 2% • **Exchanges:** 1 Starch, 1 Fat • **Carbohydrate Choices:** 1

Sweet Potato Biscuits

PREP: 10 MIN; BAKE: 12 MIN

16 to 18 biscuits

2 1/2 cups Original Bisquick mix

1/3 cup butter or margarine, softened

1 cup mashed cooked sweet potatoes

1/2 cup milk

1. Heat oven to 450°. Stir all ingredients until soft dough forms. Place dough on surface dusted with Bisquick mix; gently roll in Bisquick mix to coat. Shape into a ball; knead 3 or 4 times.

2. Roll dough 1/2 inch thick. Cut with 2 1/2-inch cutter dipped in Bisquick mix. Placc with edges touching on ungreased cookie sheet.

3. Bake 10 to 12 minutes or until golden brown. Serve warm.

High Altitude (3500 to 6500 feet): Use 3 tablespoons butter.

Betty's **TIP:** For nicely shaped biscuits, push the cutter straight down through the biscuit dough. Use any 2-inch cookie cutter to make fun or festive shapes. Or cut the dough into smaller squares, rectangles or triangles with a sharp knife that has been dipped in Bisquick mix to prevent sticking.

1 Biscuit: Calories 130 (Calories from Fat 65); Fat 7g (Saturated 4g); Cholesterol 10mg; Sodium 290mg; Carbohydrate 16g (Dietary Fiber 1g); Protein 2g • **% Daily Value:** Vitamin A 50%; Vitamin C 2%; Calcium 4%; Iron 2% • **Exchanges:** 1 Starch, 1 Fat • **Carbohydrate Choices:** 1

kids LOVE

Cheddar and Green Onion Biscuit Poppers

PREP: 8 MIN; BAKE: 9 MIN

35 to 40 biscuit poppers

2 cups Original Bisquick mix

2/3 cup milk

1/2 cup shredded Cheddar cheese (2 ounces)

4 medium green onions, sliced (1/4 cup)

2 tablespoons butter or margarine, melted

1. Heat oven to 450°. Spray cookie sheet with cooking spray. Stir Bisquick mix, milk, cheese and onions until soft dough forms.

2. Drop dough by rounded teaspoonfuls onto cookie sheet.

3. Bake 7 to 9 minutes or until golden brown. Brush butter over warm biscuits. Serve with salsa if desired.

High Altitude (3500 to 6500 feet): No changes.

Betty's **TIP:** Kids and adults alike will love the flavor and fun bite-size shape of these mini-biscuits. If you have any left over, store tightly wrapped in the freezer; warm 3 or 4 poppers at a time in the microwave on High for 20 to 30 seconds.

1 Appetizer: Calories 40 (Calories from Fat 20); Fat 2g (Saturated 1g); Cholesterol 5mg; Sodium 115mg; Carbohydrate 4g (Dietary Fiber 0g); Protein 1g • **% Daily Value:** Vitamin A 0%; Vitamin C 0%; Calcium 2%; Iron 0% • **Exchanges:** 1/2 Starch • **Carbohydrate Choices:** 0

Cheddar and Green Onion Biscuit Poppers

Easy Greek-Style Bread

PREP: 15 MIN; BAKE: 15 MIN

24 servings

1/2 cup Original Bisquick mix

1/2 cup crumbled feta cheese

1 teaspoon dried basil leaves

1 teaspoon dried oregano leaves

3 cups Original Bisquick mix

3/4 cup sun-dried tomatoes in oil, drained and chopped

1/2 cup chopped ripe olives

1 cup hot water

3 tablespoons vegetable oil

1 egg

1. Heat oven to 425°. Grease bottom and sides of rectangular pan, 13 × 9 × 2 inches, with shortening or spray with cooking spray. Stir together 1/2 cup Bisquick mix, the cheese, basil and oregano; set aside.

2. Stir remaining ingredients until moistened. Spread batter in pan; sprinkle with cheese mixture.

3. Bake 13 to 15 minutes or until golden brown. To serve, cut into 4 rows by 6 rows. Serve warm.

High Altitude (3500 to 6500 feet): No changes.

Betty's **TIP:** Homemade bread in 30 minutes? It's easy with Bisquick! This flavorful bread is a great one to serve with a special dinner, eat as a snack or enjoy for breakfast or brunch.

1 Serving: Calories 110 (Calories from Fat 50); Fat 3g (Saturated 2g); Cholesterol 10mg; Sodium 320mg; Carbohydrate 12g (Dietary Fiber 0g); Protein 2g • **% Daily Value:** Vitamin A 0%; Vitamin C 0%; Calcium 4%; Iron 4% • **Exchanges:** 1 Starch, 1 Fat • **Carbohydrate Choices:** 1

Easy Greek-Style Bread

Spinach-Cheese Bread

PREP: 15 MIN; BAKE: 1 HR 5 MIN; COOL: 20 MIN

1 loaf (16 slices)

3 cups Original Bisquick mix

1/4 cup vegetable oil

1 tablespoon caraway seed

3 eggs

1 can (11 ounces) condensed Cheddar cheese soup

1 package (10 ounces) frozen chopped spinach, thawed and squeezed to drain

1. Heat oven to 350°. Grease bottom and sides of loaf pan, 9 × 5 × 3 inches, with shortening or spray with cooking spray.

2. Stir all ingredients except spinach in large bowl until well mixed; beat with spoon 1 minute. Stir in spinach. Pour into pan.

3. Bake 55 to 65 minutes or until toothpick inserted in center comes out clean. Cool 20 minutes; remove from pan to wire rack.

High Altitude (3500 to 6500 feet): Heat oven to 375°. Add 1/4 cup all-purpose flour with the Bisquick mix. Use 2 tablespoons oil and 4 eggs. Bake 50 to 55 minutes.

Betty's **TIP:** Drain the thawed spinach in a strainer, then squeeze out the excess moisture using paper towels or a clean kitchen towel until the spinach is dry. Instead of caraway seed, use 1 tablespoon of instant minced onion to add a subtle onion flavor to the bread.

1 Slice: Calories 155 (Calories from Fat 80); Fat 9g (Saturated 2g); Cholesterol 40mg; Sodium 510mg; Carbohydrate 16g (Dietary Fiber 1g); Protein 4g • **% Daily Value:** Vitamin A 28%; Vitamin C 0%; Calcium 8%; Iron 6% • **Exchanges:** 1 Starch, 1 1/2 Fat • **Carbohydrate Choices:** 1

Spinach-Cheese Bread

kids LOVE

Orange-Blueberry Bread

PREP: 13 MIN; BAKE: 1 HR; COOL: 55 MIN

1 loaf (18 slices)

3 cups Original Bisquick mix

1/2 cup sugar

1/2 cup milk

1 tablespoon grated orange peel

3 tablespoons vegetable oil

2 eggs

1 cup fresh or frozen (rinsed and drained) blueberries

Orange Glaze (below)

Additional grated orange peel, if desired

Orange Glaze

1/2 cup powdered sugar

3 to 4 teaspoons orange juice

1. Heat oven to 350°. Grease bottom only of loaf pan, 9 × 5 × 3 inches, with shortening or spray bottom with cooking spray.

2. Stir all ingredients except blueberries, Orange Glaze and additional orange peel in large bowl until blended. Fold in blueberries. Pour into pan.

3. Bake 50 to 60 minutes or until toothpick inserted in center comes out clean. Cool 10 minutes; loosen loaf from sides of pan. Remove from pan to wire rack. Cool completely, about 45 minutes. Drizzle with Orange Glaze; sprinkle with additional orange peel.

Orange Glaze
Stir ingredients until thin enough to drizzle.

High Altitude (3500 to 6500 feet): Heat oven to 375°.

Betty's **TIP:** This bread is Bisquick at its best—moist and flavorful. Try other fruit combinations, such as lemon-raspberry or orange-cranberry. Substitute lemon peel and juice for the orange and fresh or frozen raspberries or cranberries for the blueberries.

1 Slice: Calories 155 (Calories from Fat 55); Fat 6g (Saturated 1g); Cholesterol 25mg; Sodium 300mg; Carbohydrate 23g (Dietary Fiber 0g); Protein 2g • **% Daily Value:** Vitamin A 0%; Vitamin C 0%; Calcium 4%; Iron 4% • **Exchanges:** 1 Starch, 1/2 Fruit, 1 Fat • **Carbohydrate Choices:** 1 1/2

Orange-Blueberry Bread

Cranberry-Walnut Scones

PREP: 15 MIN; BAKE: 11 MIN

12 scones

2 tablespoons water

1 cup dried cranberries

2 cups Original or Reduced Fat Bisquick mix

1/4 cup sugar

1/2 teaspoon ground cinnamon

3 tablespoons firm butter or margarine

2/3 cup buttermilk or fat-free (skim) milk

1/2 teaspoon vanilla

2/3 cup chopped walnuts

1 tablespoon butter or margarine, melted

1. Heat oven to 425°. Pour water over cranberries in 1-quart microwavable dish; cover with plastic wrap, folding back one side to vent. Microwave on High 1 minute. Uncover cranberries; cool.

2. Mix Bisquick mix, sugar and cinnamon in large bowl. Cut in 3 tablespoons butter, using pastry blender or crisscrossing 2 knives, until mixture looks like fine crumbs. Stir in buttermilk, vanilla, cranberries and walnuts just until moistened.

3. Drop dough by 1/4 cupfuls onto ungreased cookie sheet. Sprinkle with additional sugar if desired. Bake 10 to 11 minutes or until golden brown. Brush 1 tablespoon melted butter over warm scones and sprinkle with sugar if desired.

High Altitude (3500 to 6500 feet): Bake 11 to 12 minutes.

Betty's **TIP:** These flavorful scones are a hit as a warm bread for a meal or as an anytime snack. To store, wrap cooled scones tightly and freeze for up to 2 months; to reheat, microwave on High for 30 to 35 seconds.

1 Scone: Calories 215 (Calories from Fat 100); Fat 11g (Saturated 4g); Cholesterol 10mg; Sodium 320mg; Carbohydrate 26g (Dietary Fiber 1g); Protein 3g • **% Daily Value:** Vitamin A 2%; Vitamin C 0%; Calcium 6%; Iron 4% • **Exchanges:** 1 Starch, 1 Other Carbohydrate, 2 Fat • **Carbohydrate Choices:** 2

Cranberry-Walnut Scones

Cinnamon Chip–Oatmeal Muffins

PREP: 7 MIN; BAKE: 18 MIN

12 muffins

1 1/2 cups Original Bisquick mix

3/4 cup old-fashioned or quick-cooking or oats

1/3 cup packed brown sugar

2/3 cup milk

2 tablespoons vegetable oil

1 egg

1/2 cup cinnamon-flavored baking chips

1/4 cup old-fashioned or quick-cooking or oats

1. Heat oven to 400°. Line 12 medium muffin cups, 2 1/2 × 1 1/4 inches, with paper baking cups; or grease bottoms only of muffin cups with shortening.

2. Stir all ingredients except cinnamon chips and 1/4 cup oats in medium bowl just until moistened. Fold in cinnamon chips. Divide batter evenly among muffin cups. Sprinkle with 1/4 cup oats.

3. Bake 15 to 18 minutes or until toothpick inserted in center of muffin comes out clean.

High Altitude (3500 to 6500 feet): Use paper baking cups.

Betty's **TIP:** For muffins with nicely rounded tops, mix ingredients only until moistened and batter is slightly lumpy, and be sure your oven is preheated. Buttermilk lovers, you will be glad to know you can substitute buttermilk for the milk in these "oaty" muffins; it adds great flavor and moistness.

1 Muffin: Calories 180 (Calories from Fat 55); Fat 6g (Saturated 1g); Cholesterol 20mg; Sodium 230mg; Carbohydrate 28g (Dietary Fiber 1g); Protein 3g • **% Daily Value:** Vitamin A 0%; Vitamin C 0%; Calcium 4%; Iron 4% • **Exchanges:** 1 Starch, 1 Other Carbohydrate, 1 Fat • **Carbohydrate Choices:** 2

Lemon-Basil Muffins

PREP: 14 MIN; BAKE: 18 MIN

12 muffins

2 eggs

2 cups Original Bisquick mix

1/3 cup sugar

1 teaspoon grated lemon peel

1/4 cup lemon juice

1/4 cup water

2 tablespoons vegetable oil

1/2 teaspoon dried basil leaves, crumbled

1. Heat oven to 400°. Line 12 medium muffin cups, 2 1/2 × 1 1/4 inches, with paper baking cups; or grease bottoms only of muffin cups with shortening.

2. Beat eggs slightly in medium bowl. Stir in remaining ingredients just until moistened. Divide batter evenly among muffin cups.

3. Bake 15 to 18 minutes or until tops are golden brown. Remove from pan to wire rack. Serve warm.

High Altitude (3500 to 6500 feet): Use paper baking cups.

Betty's **TIP:** For best-looking muffins, bake for the shortest time stated in the recipe, then check for doneness. If the tops aren't golden brown or they don't spring back when touched lightly in the center, bake a minute or two longer and check again. For a special touch, sprinkle tops of muffins with 1/4 cup coarse white sugar crystals (decorating sugar) before baking.

1 Muffin: Calories 135 (Calories from Fat 55); Fat 6g (Saturated 1g); Cholesterol 35mg; Sodium 300mg; Carbohydrate 18g (Dietary Fiber 0g); Protein 2g • **% Daily Value:** Vitamin A 0%; Vitamin C 0%; Calcium 4%; Iron 4% • **Exchanges:** 1 Starch, 1 Fat • **Carbohydrate Choices:** 1

Chapter 3

30-MINUTE Weeknight

**Chicken-Vegetable Soup with Mini-Dumplings (page 95)
and Home-Style Beef and Potato Skillet (page 100)**

Meals

kids LOVE

Quick Italian Chicken Sandwiches
PREP: 10 MIN; COOK: 10 MIN

4 servings

4 boneless, skinless chicken breast halves (about 1 1/4 pounds)

1/2 cup Original Bisquick mix

1/2 cup grated Parmesan cheese

2 teaspoons Italian seasoning

1/2 cup water

2 tablespoons butter or margarine

4 hoagie buns, split

Lettuce leaves, if desired

4 slices (1 ounce each) fresh mozzarella cheese

1 cup spaghetti or marinara sauce, heated

1. Flatten each chicken breast half to about 1/4-inch thickness between sheets of waxed paper or plastic wrap.

2. Mix Bisquick mix, Parmesan cheese and Italian seasoning. Dip chicken into water, then coat with Bisquick mixture.

3. Melt butter in 12-inch nonstick skillet over medium heat. Cook chicken in butter 8 to 10 minutes, turning once, until no longer pink in center. Fill buns with chicken, lettuce, mozzarella cheese and spaghetti sauce.

High Altitude (3500 to 6500 feet): No changes.

Betty's **TIP:** Dip chicken into red wine vinegar instead of the water for a zesty Italian taste. If you don't have Italian seasoning, you can use instead 1/2 teaspoon each of dried basil, marjoram, oregano and thyme leaves.

1 Sandwich: Calories 590 (Calories from Fat 190); Fat 21g (Saturated 10g); Cholesterol 110mg; Sodium 1350mg; Carbohydrate 55g (Dietary Fiber 3); Protein 45g • % **Daily Value:** Vitamin A 16%; Vitamin C 8%; Calcium 44%; Iron 20% • **Exchanges:** 3 1/2 Starch, 5 Lean Meat, 1 Fat • **Carbohydrate Choices:** 3 1/2

Quick Italian Chicken Sandwiches

Chicken and Biscuits

PREP: 15 MIN; BAKE: 10 MIN; COOK: 10 MIN

6 servings

Drop Biscuits (below)

1 tablespoon vegetable oil

1 1/2 teaspoons chopped fresh or 1/2 teaspoon dried thyme leaves

1/4 teaspoon pepper

1 1/4 pounds boneless, skinless chicken breasts, cut into 1-inch pieces

1/2 teaspoon Dijon mustard

1 bag (1 pound) frozen mixed vegetables

1 container (10 ounces) refrigerated Alfredo pasta sauce

Drop Biscuits

2 1/4 cups Original Bisquick mix

2/3 cup milk

1. Make Drop Biscuits. While biscuits are baking, heat oil, thyme and pepper in 10-inch nonstick skillet over medium-high heat. Cook chicken in oil mixture, stirring occasionally, until no longer pink in center.

2. Stir in remaining ingredients; reduce heat to medium. Cover and cook 5 to 6 minutes, stirring occasionally, until hot.

3. Split biscuits; serve chicken mixture over biscuits.

Drop Biscuits

Heat oven to 450°. Stir ingredients until soft dough forms. Drop by 6 spoonfuls onto ungreased cookie sheet. Bake 8 to 10 minutes or until golden brown.

High Altitude (3500 to 6500 feet): Thaw frozen vegetables before adding to skillet.

Betty's **TIP:** It's easy to make special-shaped biscuits. Make Drop Biscuits as directed—except knead dough on surface dusted with Bisquick mix 10 times. Roll dough 1/2 inch thick. Cut with any shaped cutter; bake as directed.

1 Serving: Calories 505 (Calories from Fat 250); Fat 28g (Saturated 13g); Cholesterol 100mg; Sodium 940mg; Carbohydrate 36g (Dietary Fiber 3g); Protein 27g • **% Daily Value:** Vitamin A 56%; Vitamin C 30%; Calcium 40%; Iron 18% • **Exchanges:** 2 Starch, 1 Vegetable, 3 Lean Meat, 3 1/2 Fat • **Carbohydrate Choices:** 2 1/2

Mou Shu Chicken

PREP: 7 MIN; COOK: 20 MIN

6 servings

1 tablespoon vegetable oil

1 bag (16 ounces) coleslaw mix

1 package (8 ounces) sliced mushrooms

2 cups shredded cooked chicken

1 tablespoon grated gingerroot

3 tablespoons hoisin sauce

1 1/4 cups Original Bisquick mix

1 1/4 cups milk

1 egg

Green onions, chopped, if desired

1. Heat oil in 4-quart Dutch oven over medium-high heat. Cook coleslaw mix, mushrooms, chicken and gingerroot in oil about 10 minutes, stirring frequently, until vegetables are tender. Stir in hoisin sauce. Reduce heat; keep warm.

2. Stir Bisquick mix, milk and egg in medium bowl until blended. Stir in onions.

3. Lightly spray 10-inch skillet with cooking spray; heat over medium-high heat. Pour slightly less than 1/4 cup batter into skillet; rotate skillet to make a thin pancake, 5 to 6 inches in diameter. Cook until bubbles break on surface; turn. Cook other side until golden brown. Keep warm while making remaining pancakes.

4. Spoon about 1/2 cup vegetable mixture onto each pancake; roll up.

High Altitude (3500 to 6500 feet): Cook pancakes in 10-inch nonstick skillet.

Betty's **TIP:** Add an extra spark of color and flavor by stirring in half of a red bell pepper, thinly sliced, with the coleslaw, mushrooms and chicken. One clove of garlic, finely chopped, can also be added with the vegetables for additional flavor.

1 Serving: Calories 295 (Calories from Fat 100); Fat 12g (Saturated 3g); Cholesterol 80mg; Sodium 570mg; Carbohydrate 27g (Dietary Fiber 3g); Protein 20g • **% Daily Value:** Vitamin A 4%; Vitamin C 12%; Calcium 8%; Iron 8% • **Exchanges:** 1 1/2 Starch, 1 Vegetable, 2 Medium-Fat Meat • **Carbohydrate Choices:** 2

Sweet-and-Sour Chicken Crepes

PREP: 20 MIN; COOK: 6 MIN

4 servings (2 crepes each)

Crepes (below)

2 cups frozen stir-fry bell peppers and onions (from 1-pound bag), thawed and drained

1 cup cut-up cooked chicken

1 can (8 ounces) pineapple tidbits or chunks, drained

2/3 cup sweet-and-sour sauce

Crepes

1 cup Original Bisquick mix

3/4 cup milk

1 teaspoon soy sauce

1 egg

1. Make Crepes.

2. Heat stir-fry vegetables, chicken, pineapple and 1/3 cup of the sweet-and-sour sauce in 2-quart saucepan over medium-high heat, stirring constantly, until hot.

3. Spoon about 2 tablespoons filling onto each crepe. Roll up; carefully place seam side down. Heat remaining 1/3 cup sweet-and-sour sauce until hot. Serve over crepes.

Crepes

Stir all ingredients until blended. Lightly spray 6- or 7-inch skillet with cooking spray; heat over medium-high heat. For each crepe, pour 2 tablespoons batter into hot skillet; rotate skillet until batter covers bottom. Cook until golden brown. Gently loosen edge with metal spatula; turn and cook other side until golden brown. Stack crepes as you remove them from skillet, placing waxed paper between them. Keep crepes covered to prevent them from drying out.

High Altitude (3500 to 6500 feet): No changes.

Betty's **TIP:** Make the crepes ahead of time. Stack crepes with waxed paper between them, place them in a plastic bag (so they won't dry out) and refrigerate. At suppertime, make the filling and quickly reheat the crepes in the microwave on High for 30 seconds. Assemble and serve.

1 Serving: Calories 325 (Calories from Fat 90); Fat 10g (Saturated 3g); Cholesterol 85mg; Sodium 730mg; Carbohydrate 43g (Dietary Fiber 3g); Protein 16g • **% Daily Value:** Vitamin A 8%; Vitamin C 38%; Calcium 14%; Iron 12% • **Exchanges:** 2 Starch, 1/2 Fruit, 1 Vegetable, 1 Medium-Fat Meat, 1 Fat • **Carbohydrate Choices:** 3

Sweet-and-Sour Chicken Crepes

Cheesy Chicken Casserole

PREP: 10 MIN; BAKE: 22 MIN

6 servings

2 cups cut-up cooked chicken

1 jar (16 ounces) Cheddar cheese pasta sauce

1 bag (1 pound) frozen broccoli, carrots and cauliflower, thawed and drained

1 1/4 cups Original Bisquick mix

1/4 cup grated Parmesan cheese

1/4 cup firm butter or margarine

1 egg, slightly beaten

1. Heat oven to 400°. Mix chicken, pasta sauce and vegetables. Pour into ungreased square pan, 9 × 9 × 2 inches.

2. Mix Bisquick mix, Parmesan cheese and butter with fork or pastry blender until crumbly. Stir in egg. Sprinkle over chicken mixture.

3. Bake uncovered 20 to 22 minutes or until topping is light golden brown.

High Altitude (3500 to 6500 feet): Heat chicken, pasta sauce and vegetables in 3-quart saucepan over medium heat, stirring occasionally, until hot and bubbly before pouring into square pan.

Betty's **TIP:** Using frozen cooked chicken, thawed, or two 5-ounce cans of chunk chicken, drained, will give you a head start on this casserole. A 16-ounce jar of purchased Alfredo pasta sauce can be used in place of the Cheddar cheese sauce for a change of flavor.

1 Serving: Calories 490 (Calories from Fat 280); Fat 31g (Saturated 15g); Cholesterol 130mg; Sodium 1030mg; Carbohydrate 25g (Dietary Fiber 3g); Protein 28g • **% Daily Value:** Vitamin A 58%; Vitamin C 28%; Calcium 22%; Iron 12% • **Exchanges:** 2 Starch, 3 Medium-Fat Meat, 2 Fat • **Carbohydrate Choices:** 1 1/2

Lemon-Ginger Chicken

PREP: 15 MIN; COOK: 10 MIN

4 servings

4 boneless, skinless chicken breast
  halves (about 1 1/4 pounds)
1/2 cup Original Bisquick mix
1/4 cup plain bread crumbs
1 tablespoon grated lemon peel
1/2 teaspoon grated gingerroot
1/2 cup water
3 tablespoons vegetable oil
Lemon Sauce (below)
Lemon slices, if desired

Lemon Sauce

1/4 cup lemon juice
1/4 cup water
3 tablespoons sugar
1 tablespoon cornstarch
1/4 teaspoon grated gingerroot
1 drop yellow food color,
  if desired

1. Flatten each chicken breast half to about 1/4-inch thickness between sheets of waxed paper or plastic wrap.

2. Mix Bisquick mix, bread crumbs, lemon peel and gingerroot. Pour water into shallow glass or plastic bowl. Dip chicken into water, then coat with Bisquick mixture.

3. Heat oil in 12-inch nonstick skillet over medium heat. Cook chicken in oil 8 to 10 minutes, turning once, until no longer pink in center.

4. While chicken is cooking, make Lemon Sauce; pour over chicken. Garnish with lemon slices.

Lemon Sauce
Mix all ingredients in 1-quart saucepan. Heat over medium heat, stirring occasionally, until thickened and bubbly.

High Altitude (3500 to 6500 feet): Cook chicken in oil 11 to 13 minutes or until meat thermometer inserted in center of chicken reads 170°.

Betty's **TIP:** Flatten chicken breasts by pounding with a meat mallet, rolling pin or even the heel of your hand. Thinner chicken breasts cook more evenly and quickly; so it's a good step to take time to flatten them, even when you're short on time.

1 Serving: Calories 375 (Calories from Fat 155); Fat 17g (Saturated 3g); Cholesterol 75mg; Sodium 340mg; Carbohydrate 27g (Dietary Fiber 0g); Protein 29g • **% Daily Value:** Vitamin A 0%; Vitamin C 4%; Calcium 6%; Iron 10% • **Exchanges:** 2 Starch, 2 Lean Meat, 2 Fat • **Carbohydrate Choices:** 2

ULTIMATE Chicken Pot Pie

PREP: 15 MIN; BAKE: 40 MIN; STAND: 5 MIN

6 servings

1 package (16 ounces) frozen mixed vegetables

1 cup cut-up cooked chicken

1 jar (12 ounces) chicken gravy

2 cups shredded Wisconsin Cheddar cheese (8 ounces)

1 cup Original Bisquick mix

1/4 cup milk

1/4 cup dried thyme leaves

2 eggs

1. Heat oven to 375°. Heat vegetables, chicken and gravy to boiling in 2-quart saucepan, stirring frequently; keep warm.

2. Stir cheese, Bisquick, milk, thyme leaves and eggs with a fork until blended. Pour chicken mixture into ungreased 2-quart casserole. Pour batter over chicken mixture.

3. Bake 35 to 40 minutes or until crust is golden brown. Let stand 5 minutes before serving.

High Altitude (3500 to 6500 feet): No changes needed.

Betty's **TIP:** If you have leftover cooked vegetables, you can substitute them for the frozen vegetables.

1 Serving: Calories 365 (Calories from Fat 180); Fat 20g (Saturated 10g); Cholesterol 130mg; Sodium 940mg; Carbohydrate 25g (Dietary Fiber 4g); Protein 25g • **% Daily Value:** Vitamin A 16%; Vitamin C 4%; Calcium 28%; Iron 16% • **Exchanges:** 1 1/2 Starch, 3 Medium-Fat Meat, 1/2 Fat • **Carbohydrate Choices:** 1 1/2

Ultimate Chicken Pot Pie

Chili-Coated Chicken Drummies

PREP: 10 MIN; MICROWAVE: 19 MIN

4 servings

1/2 cup Original Bisquick mix

2 tablespoons yellow cornmeal

2 teaspoons chili powder

1 teaspoon paprika

1/2 teaspoon salt

1/8 teaspoon pepper

8 chicken drumsticks, thighs or wings (about 2 pounds)

1. Mix all ingredients except chicken in 2-quart resealable plastic food-storage bag.

2. Shake 2 pieces of chicken at a time in bag until coated. Arrange chicken, skin sides up and thickest parts to outside edge, in ungreased 9-inch microwavable pie plate.

3. Cover with waxed paper. Microwave on High 10 minutes. Turn pie plate 1/2 turn. Microwave 6 to 9 minutes longer or until juice of chicken is no longer pink when centers of thickest pieces are cut.

High Altitude (3500 to 6500 feet): No changes.

Betty's **TIP:** Using all of the same kind of chicken pieces helps to cook the chicken evenly, which is especially important for microwave cooking. To check if it's fully cooked through, cut into the chicken with a sharp knife; the juices should be clear, not pink.

1 Serving: Calories 275 (Calories from Fat 115); Fat 13g (Saturated 4g); Cholesterol 85mg; Sodium 600mg; Carbohydrate 13g (Dietary Fiber 1g); Protein 30g • % **Daily Value:** Vitamin A 18%; Vitamin C 0%; Calcium 6%; Iron 16% • **Exchanges:** 1 Starch, 4 Lean Meat • **Carbohydrate Choices:** 1

kids
LOVE

Chicken-Vegetable Soup
with Mini-Dumplings

PREP: 7 MIN; COOK: 25 MIN

Photo on page 82

6 servings (1 cup each)

2 cups cut-up cooked chicken

4 cups chicken broth

1 tablespoon chopped fresh
   parsley

1 tablespoon chopped fresh
   thyme leaves

2 cloves garlic, finely chopped

1 bag (1 pound) frozen mixed
   vegetables or soup vegetables,
   thawed and drained

1 cup Original Bisquick mix

1/3 cup milk

1. Heat all ingredients except Bisquick mix and milk to boiling in 3-quart saucepan.

2. Stir Bisquick mix and milk until soft dough forms. Drop dough by teaspoonfuls onto boiling soup. If dumplings sink into soup, carefully bring them to top of broth using slotted spoon. Reduce heat to low.

3. Cook uncovered 10 minutes. Cover and cook 10 minutes longer.

High Altitude (3500 to 6500 feet): No changes.

Betty's **TIP:** The mini-dumplings cook in much less time than regular-size dumplings. When you're cooking in a hurry, thinking smaller can save you time.

1 Serving: Calories 215 (Calories from Fat 65); Fat 7g (Saturated 2g); Cholesterol 40mg; Sodium 1030mg; Carbohydrate 18g (Dietary Fiber 2g); Protein 20g • **% Daily Value:** Vitamin A 42%; Vitamin C 20%; Calcium 8%; Iron 10% • **Exchanges:** 1/2 Starch, 2 Vegetable, 2 1/2 Lean Meat • **Carbohydrate Choices:** 1

Corn Bread Chili Stacks

PREP: 10 MIN; BAKE: 20 MIN

4 servings

3/4 cup yellow cornmeal

2/3 cup Original Bisquick mix

3/4 cup buttermilk

2 tablespoons butter or margarine, melted

1 egg

1 can (15 ounces) spicy chili

1 can (14 1/2 ounces) diced tomatoes with mild green chilies, undrained

1 cup cut-up cooked chicken

4 slices American cheese, cut diagonally in half, if desired

1. Heat oven to 450°. Spray bottom and sides of square pan, 8 × 8 × 2 inches, with cooking spray. Stir cornmeal, Bisquick mix, buttermilk, butter and egg in medium bowl until blended. Pour into pan.

2. Bake uncovered 18 to 20 minutes or until toothpick inserted in center comes out clean. Meanwhile, heat chili, tomatoes and chicken in 2-quart saucepan over medium heat, stirring occasionally, until bubbly.

3. Cut corn bread into 4 squares; split each square horizontally. Fill with 1/2 cup chili mixture and cheese slice.

High Altitude (3500 to 6500 feet): No changes.

Betty's **TIP:** To add color and flavor, add strips of red, yellow or green bell pepper on top of cheese slices when making stacks. Finish with a dollop of sour cream.

1 Serving: Calories 420 (Calories from Fat 130); Fat 14g (Saturated 6g); Cholesterol 100mg; Sodium 900mg; Carbohydrate 52g (Dietary Fiber 6g); Protein 22g • **% Daily Value:** Vitamin A 20%; Vitamin C 12%; Calcium 16%; Iron 24% • **Exchanges:** 3 Starch, 2 Vegetable, 2 Lean Meat • **Carbohydrate Choices:** 4

Salsa Beef Biscuit Bake

PREP: 10 MIN; BAKE: 20 MIN

6 servings

1 pound ground beef

1 jar (16 ounces) thick 'n chunky salsa

2 cups Original Bisquick mix

3/4 cup milk

1 medium green onion, chopped (1 tablespoon)

1 cup shredded Cheddar cheese (4 ounces)

1. Heat oven to 400°. Spray bottom and sides of square pan, 9 × 9 × 2 inches, with cooking spray. Cook beef in 10-inch skillet over medium-high heat, about 8 minutes, stirring occasionally, until brown; drain. Stir in salsa. Spread beef mixture in pan.

2. Stir Bisquick mix, milk, onion and cheese until soft dough forms. Drop dough by 12 tablespoonfuls over beef mixture.

3. Bake uncovered about 20 minutes or until golden brown and toothpick inserted in biscuits comes out clean.

High Altitude (3500 to 6500 feet): Use 2 1/4 cups Bisquick mix. Bake about 27 minutes.

Betty's **TIP:** Ground turkey can be used instead of beef in this quick and easy bake. Garnish with the works—chopped tomatoes, chopped avocado and sour cream!

1 Serving: Calories 420 (Calories from Fat 205); Fat 23g (Saturated 10g); Cholesterol 65mg; Sodium 1060mg; Carbohydrate 30g (Dietary Fiber 2g); Protein 23g • **% Daily Value:** Vitamin A 16%; Vitamin C 8%; Calcium 22%; Iron 18% • **Exchanges:** 2 Starch, 2 High-Fat Meat, 1 Fat • **Carbohydrate Choices:** 2

Southwestern Beef on Biscuits

PREP: 3 MIN; BAKE: 14 MIN; COOK: 14 MIN

10 servings

Biscuits (below)

1 tub (32 ounces) refrigerated barbeque sauce with sliced cooked beef

1 can (11 ounces) whole kernel corn with red and green peppers, drained

1 can (2 1/4 ounces) sliced ripe olives, drained

1/2 cup shredded Cheddar or Colby cheese (2 ounces)

1/3 cup sour cream

Biscuits

3 1/4 cups Original Bisquick mix

1 cup milk

1. Make Biscuits.

2. While biscuits are baking, heat beef mixture in 4-quart saucepan over medium heat 10 to 12 minutes, stirring occasionally, until hot. Stir in corn and olives; heat until hot.

3. Split warm biscuits; place 1 half biscuit, cut side up, on each serving plate. Spoon beef mixture over biscuit halves. Sprinkle with cheese. Top with sour cream.

Biscuits

Heat oven to 450°. Stir ingredients until soft dough forms. Place on surface dusted with Bisquick mix. Knead 10 times. Roll dough 1/2 inch thick. Cut with 4-inch cutter to make 5 biscuits. Place on ungreased cookie sheet. Bake 11 to 14 minutes or until golden brown.

High Altitude (3500 to 6500 feet): No changes.

Betty's **TIP:** Turn this easy dish into a weeknight fiesta with additional toppings such as shredded lettuce, chopped tomatoes, sliced green onions and guacamole.

1 Serving: Calories 430 (Calories from Fat 200); Fat 22g (Saturated 6g); Cholesterol 40mg; Sodium 1310mg; Carbohydrate 34g (Dietary Fiber 2g); Protein 26g • **% Daily Value:** Vitamin A 8%; Vitamin C 4%; Calcium 14%; Iron 16% • **Exchanges:** 2 Starch, 3 Medium-Fat Meat, 1 Fat • **Carbohydrate Choices:** 2

Southwestern Beef on Biscuits

Home-Style Beef and Potato Skillet

PREP: 10 MIN; COOK: 18 MIN

Photo on page 83

5 servings

1 pound ground beef

4 medium green onions, chopped (1/4 cup)

1 cup water

1 envelope (0.87 ounce) onion gravy mix

2 cups frozen diced potatoes with onions and peppers

1/2 cup frozen baby sweet peas (from 1-pound bag)

1 large tomato, chopped (1 cup)

1 1/2 cups Original Bisquick mix

1/2 cup water

1. Cook beef in 10-inch skillet over medium-high heat, about 8 minutes, stirring occasionally, until brown; drain. Stir in 2 tablespoons of the onions, 1 cup water and the gravy mix (dry). Cook, stirring constantly, until mixture thickens. Stir in potatoes, peas and tomato. Heat until hot; reduce heat to medium-low.

2. Stir Bisquick mix, remaining 2 tablespoons onions and 1/2 cup water until soft dough forms.

3. Drop dough by tablespoonfuls onto beef mixture. Cover and cook 8 minutes. Cook uncovered 8 to 10 minutes longer or until toothpick inserted in center of dumplings comes out clean.

High Altitude (3500 to 6500 feet): No changes.

Betty's **TIP:** A great way to drop the dough into dumplings is to use a small cookie-dough scoop; it makes it easy to quickly drop round, even-sized dumplings onto the beef mixture.

1 Serving: Calories 410 (Calories from Fat 170); Fat 19g (Saturated 7g); Cholesterol 50mg; Sodium 850mg; Carbohydrate 38g (Dietary Fiber 3g); Protein 22g • **% Daily Value:** Vitamin A 10%; Vitamin C 22%; Calcium 10%; Iron 20% • **Exchanges:** 2 1/2 Starch, 2 High-Fat Meat, 1 Fat • **Carbohydrate Choices:** 2 1/2

Southwest Beef Empanadas

PREP: 15 MIN; BAKE: 15 MIN

8 servings

1 pound ground beef

1 envelope (1.25-ounce size) taco seasoning mix

2/3 cup water

1 cup refrigerated loose-pack hash brown potatoes

1 can (8 1/4 ounces) julienne or sliced carrots, drained

1 tablespoon instant minced onion

4 1/2 cups Original Bisquick mix

1 cup boiling water

1. Heat oven to 400°. Spray cookie sheet with cooking spray. Cook beef in 10-inch skillet over medium-high heat, about 8 minutes, stirring occasionally, until brown; drain. Stir in taco seasoning mix, 2/3 cup water, the potatoes, carrots and onion. Heat beef mixture over medium heat 5 minutes.

2. Stir Bisquick mix and boiling water until dough forms. Place dough on surface sprinkled with Bisquick mix; roll in Bisquick mix to coat. Knead 20 times. Divide dough into 6 balls. Pat or roll each ball into 7-inch circle. Place on cookie sheet.

3. Spoon about 1/2 cup beef mixture onto half of each circle. Moisten edge of circle. Fold circle over beef mixture; press edge with fork to seal. Cut 2 small slits in top of each crust to allow steam to escape. Bake about 15 minutes or until light golden brown.

High Altitude (3500 to 6500 feet): No changes.

Betty's **TIP:** For a special touch, use mini cookie cutters or canapé cutters to cut decorative holes in the top of each crust, rather than cutting 2 small slits, in these tasty Southwest meat- and vegetable-filled breads. Serve with salsa for extra punch!

1 Serving: Calories 440 (Calories from Fat 160); Fat 18g (Saturated 6g); Cholesterol 30mg; Sodium 1240mg; Carbohydrate 53g (Dietary Fiber 2g); Protein 16g · **% Daily Value:** Vitamin A 82%; Vitamin C 4%; Calcium 14%; Iron 18% · **Exchanges:** 3 1/2 Starch, 1 High-Fat Meat, 1 1/2 Fat · **Carbohydrate Choices:** 3 1/2

Mini Barbecued Meat Loaves

PREP: 8 MIN; BAKE: 22 MIN

6 servings

1/2 cup barbecue sauce

1 pound lean ground beef

1/2 pound ground pork

1/2 cup Original Bisquick mix

1/4 teaspoon pepper

1 small onion, finely chopped
(1/4 cup)

1 egg

1. Heat oven to 450°.

2. Reserve 1/4 cup of the barbecue sauce. Mix remaining ingredients and 1/4 cup barbecue sauce. Place meat mixture in ungreased rectangular pan, 13 × 9 × 2 inches; pat into 12 × 4-inch rectangle. Cut lengthwise down center and then crosswise into sixths to form 12 loaves. Separate loaves slightly. Brush loaves with reserved 1/4 cup barbecue sauce.

3. Bake 18 to 22 minutes or until loaves are no longer pink in center, juice is clear and meat thermometer reads 160° when inserted in center of loaves.

High Altitude (3500 to 6500 feet): No changes.

Betty's **TIP:** Offering individual loaves makes kids feel special and makes meat loaf an easy homemade dinner idea for a weeknight meal. If you prefer all ground beef in your meat loaf, you can use 1 1/2 pounds ground beef instead of the beef-and-pork mixture in these tasty loaves.

1 Serving: Calories 305 (Calories from Fat 160); Fat 18g (Saturated 7g); Cholesterol 100mg; Sodium 410mg; Carbohydrate 14g (Dietary Fiber 0g); Protein 22g • **% Daily Value:** Vitamin A 2%; Vitamin C 0%; Calcium 4%; Iron 12% • **Exchanges:** 1 Starch, 3 Medium-Fat Meat • **Carbohydrate Choices:** 1

Mini Barbecued Meat Loaves

Almond- and Peach-Crusted Pork Chops

PREP: 10 MIN; COOK: 18 MIN

6 servings

1 egg

2 tablespoons peach preserves

1/2 cup Original Bisquick mix

1/2 cup coarsely chopped sliced
  almonds

1 tablespoon cornmeal

1/2 teaspoon salt

6 pork boneless loin chops,
  1/2 inch thick (1 1/2 pounds)

1 tablespoon vegetable oil

Chopped fresh parsley, if desired

1. Beat egg and preserves in shallow dish with fork, breaking apart any large pieces of preserves. Mix Bisquick mix, almonds, cornmeal and salt in another shallow dish. Dip pork chops into egg mixture, then coat with Bisquick mixture.

2. Heat oil in 12-inch nonstick skillet over medium-low heat. Cook pork chops in oil 15 to 18 minutes, turning once, until crust is golden brown and pork is slightly pink in center. Sprinkle with parsley. Serve immediately.

High Altitude (3500 to 6500 feet): No changes.

Betty's **TIP:** An extra-easy dress-up for these moist chops is to heat additional peach preserves until melted and drizzle over the chops. Apricot preserves can be substituted for the peach preserves.

1 Serving: Calories 315 (Calories from Fat 155); Fat 17g (Saturated 4g); Cholesterol 90mg; Sodium 340mg; Carbohydrate 14g (Dietary Fiber 2g); Protein 27g • **% Daily Value:** Vitamin A 0%; Vitamin C 0%; Calcium 4%; Iron 8% • **Exchanges:** 1 Starch, 3 1/2 Lean Meat, 1 Fat • **Carbohydrate Choices:** 1

Almond- and Peach-Crusted Pork Chops

Italian Pork Chops

PREP: 5 MIN; COOK: 20 MIN

4 servings

4 pork loin chops, 1/2 inch thick
   (1 1/2 pounds)

1/2 cup Original Bisquick mix

1/3 cup Italian dressing

1/2 cup garlic-herb dry bread
   crumbs

2 tablespoons vegetable oil

1. Coat pork chops with Bisquick mix. Dip coated pork into dressing, then coat with bread crumbs.

2. Heat oil in 12-inch nonstick skillet over medium-high heat. Cook pork in oil about 5 minutes or until golden brown; reduce heat to low. Carefully turn pork. Cook 10 to 15 minutes longer or until pork is slightly pink when cut near bone. Serve immediately.

High Altitude (3500 to 6500 feet): No changes.

Betty's **TIP:** You can use boneless pork chops if you prefer; you may have some leftover coating ingredients. Make it super simple by serving these savory pork chops with cooked broccoli, carrot sticks and whole-grain rolls. Dessert? Cookies or ice cream!

1 Serving: Calories 400 (Calories from Fat 215); Fat 24g (Saturated 5g); Cholesterol 68mg; Sodium 470mg; Carbohydrate 20g (Dietary Fiber 0g); Protein 26g • **% Daily Value:** Vitamin A 0%; Vitamin C 0%; Calcium 6%; Iron 10% • **Exchanges:** 1 Starch, 3 High-Fat Meat • **Carbohydrate Choices:** 1

Black Beans and Ham

PREP: 15 MIN; COOK: 15 MIN

6 servings

1 tablespoon vegetable oil

1 large onion, chopped (1 cup)

1/2 cup chopped red or green bell pepper

2 cans (15 ounces each) black beans, undrained

2 cups cubed fully cooked ham (12 ounces)

2 teaspoons chili powder

1 1/2 cups Original Bisquick mix

1/3 cup cornmeal

2/3 cup milk

1/2 cup shredded Cheddar cheese (2 ounces)

1. Heat oil in 4-quart Dutch oven over medium heat. Cook onion and bell pepper in oil, stirring occasionally, until tender. Stir in beans, ham and 1 teaspoon of the chili powder. Heat to boiling; reduce heat to low.

2. Stir remaining 1 teaspoon chili powder, the Bisquick mix, cornmeal and milk until soft dough forms. Drop by 6 spoonfuls onto simmering bean mixture.

3. Cook uncovered 10 minutes. Cover and cook 5 minutes longer. Sprinkle with cheese. Cover and let stand until cheese is melted.

High Altitude (3500 to 6500 feet): After dropping dough onto bean mixture, cook uncovered over medium-low heat 12 minutes. Cover and cook 10 minutes longer. Sprinkle with cheese. Cover and cook 2 minutes.

Betty's **TIP:** Pinto beans or a combination of black and pinto beans will give a slightly different twist to this dish. A southern-inspired meal, this ham and black bean casserole has a subtle spicy taste and cornmeal dumplings. Serve with cooked greens or okra and iced tea for a complete southern theme.

1 Serving: Calories 470 (Calories from Fat 135); Fat 15g (Saturated 5g); Cholesterol 40mg; Sodium 1720mg; Carbohydrate 66g (Dietary Fiber 11g); Protein 29g • **% Daily Value:** Vitamin A 24%; Vitamin C 22%; Calcium 24%; Iron 30% • **Exchanges:** 4 1/2 Starch, 1 1/2 Medium-Fat Meat • **Carbohydrate Choices:** 4 1/2

Ham and Swiss Cheese Bake

PREP: 14 MIN; BAKE: 16 MIN

8 servings

2 cups Original Bisquick mix

1/3 cup honey mustard

1/3 cup milk

2 cups cubed fully cooked ham
(12 ounces)

4 medium green onions, sliced
(1/4 cup)

1/4 cup chopped red bell pepper

1/4 cup sour cream

1 cup shredded Swiss cheese
(4 ounces)

1. Heat oven to 450°. Spray bottom and sides of rectangular pan, 13 × 9 × 2 inches, with cooking spray. Stir Bisquick mix, mustard and milk until soft dough forms; press in bottom of pan. Bake 8 to 10 minutes or until crust is golden brown.

2. Mix ham, onions, bell pepper and sour cream; spread over crust. Sprinkle with cheese.

3. Bake uncovered 5 to 6 minutes or until mixture is hot and cheese is melted.

High Altitude (3500 to 6500 feet): Increase bake time in step 3 to 6 to 7 minutes.

Betty's **TIP:** To round out your meal, add steamed broccoli or carrots and some simple fresh-fruit kabobs. For extra eye appeal, garnish this quick homemade supper with bell pepper rings.

1 Serving: Calories 265 (Calories from Fat 115); Fat 13g (Saturated 5g); Cholesterol 40mg; Sodium 1160mg; Carbohydrate 24g (Dietary Fiber 1g); Protein 14g • **% Daily Value:** Vitamin A 10%; Vitamin C 8%; Calcium 22%; Iron 8% • **Exchanges:** 1 1/2 Starch, 1 1/2 High-Fat Meat • **Carbohydrate Choices:** 1 1/2

Ham and Swiss Cheese Bake

Ham Chowder with Rolled Parmesan Biscuits

PREP: 5 MIN; BAKE: 10 MIN; COOK: 15 MIN

8 servings

Rolled Parmesan Biscuits (below)

2 cans (10 3/4 ounces each) condensed cream of potato soup

1 can (11 ounces) whole kernel corn, drained

3 small red potatoes, cut into 1/8-inch slices

1 medium stalk celery, sliced (1/2 cup)

1 cup diced fully cooked ham (6 ounces)

1 3/4 cups milk

Rolled Parmesan Biscuits

2 1/4 cups Original Bisquick mix

1/4 cup grated Parmesan cheese

2/3 cup milk

1. Make Rolled Parmesan Biscuits.

2. While biscuits are baking, cook remaining ingredients in 10-inch nonstick skillet over medium-high heat about 15 minutes, stirring occasionally, until potatoes are tender.

3. Ladle each serving of chowder over a biscuit.

Rolled Parmesan Biscuits

Heat oven to 450°. Stir all ingredients until soft dough forms. Place dough on surface sprinkled with Bisquick mix. Knead 10 times. Roll dough 1/2 inch thick. Cut with 2 1/2-inch cutter. Place about 1 inch apart on ungreased cookie sheet. Brush with additional milk and sprinkle with additional Parmesan cheese if desired. Bake 8 to 10 minutes or until golden brown.

High Altitude (3500 to 6500 feet): Heat ingredients in step 2 to boiling over medium-high heat; reduce heat. Cover and simmer 25 to 30 minutes, stirring every 2 to 3 minutes, until potatoes are tender.

Betty's **TIP:** You can use two 10 3/4-ounce cans of ready-to-eat cream of potato soup instead of the condensed soup; decrease the milk to 1/2 cup. Clam chowder would also taste great served over these special Parmesan biscuits. Use 2 cans of clam chowder instead of the potato soup, and omit the ham.

1 Serving: Calories 330 (Calories from Fat 90); Fat 10g (Saturated 4g); Cholesterol 20mg; Sodium 1460mg; Carbohydrate 50g (Dietary Fiber 3g); Protein 13g • **% Daily Value:** Vitamin A 4%; Vitamin C 8%; Calcium 22%; Iron 12% • **Exchanges:** 2 1/2 Starch, 1 Skim Milk, 1 Fat • **Carbohydrate Choices:** 3

Seafood à la King

PREP: 15 MIN; BAKE: 10 MIN

6 servings

2 1/4 cups Original or Reduced Fat Bisquick mix

3/4 cup fat-free (skim) milk

1 can (18.5 ounces) ready-to-serve New England clam chowder

1 cup frozen mixed vegetables (from 1-pound bag)

1 package (5 ounces) frozen cooked salad shrimp, thawed and drained

1 tablespoon Original Bisquick mix

1 teaspoon dried dill weed

1/8 teaspoon pepper

1. Heat oven to 450°. Stir 2 1/4 cups Bisquick mix and the milk until soft dough forms. Drop by 6 spoonfuls onto ungreased cookie sheet. Bake about 10 minutes or until golden brown.

2. While biscuits are baking, mix remaining ingredients in 2-quart saucepan. Heat to boiling over medium heat, stirring occasionally.

3. To serve, split biscuits in half. Spoon generous 1/4 cup hot chowder mixture over bottom of each biscuit. Top with remaining biscuit halves. Spoon 1/4 cup chowder mixture over top of each biscuit.

High Altitude (3500 to 6500 feet): No changes.

Betty's **TIP:** You can make both the biscuits and the seafood chowder ahead. Store baked biscuits at room temperature, then warm in the oven or microwave. Refrigerate chowder until serving time, then reheat. If you don't like shrimp, use instead a 6-ounce can of skinless boneless salmon or tuna, drained.

1 Serving: Calories 315 (Calories from Fat 110); Fat 12g (Saturated 3g); Cholesterol 50mg; Sodium 1140mg; Carbohydrate 39g (Dietary Fiber 3g); Protein 13g • % **Daily Value:** Vitamin A 30%; Vitamin C 4%; Calcium 10%; Iron 26% • **Exchanges:** 3 Starch, 1 Medium-Fat Meat • **Carbohydrate Choices:** 2 1/2

Salmon Patties

PREP: 15 MIN; COOK: 12 MIN

4 servings

1 cup soft bread crumbs (about
   1 1/2 slices bread)

8 medium green onions,
   finely chopped (1/2 cup)

1/2 cup Original or Reduced Fat
   Bisquick mix

1 tablespoon Dijon mustard

1/4 teaspoon pepper

2 eggs, slightly beaten

1 can (14 3/4 ounces) red salmon,
   drained and flaked

2 tablespoons butter or margarine

1/2 cup dill dip

1. Stir together all ingredients except butter and dill dip. Shape mixture into 4 patties, using a heaping 1/2 cupful for each patty.

2. Melt butter in 10-inch nonstick skillet over medium heat. Cook patties in butter 10 to 12 minutes, turning once, until brown and cooked through. Serve with dill dip.

High Altitude (3500 to 6500 feet): No changes.

Betty's **TIP:** If you can't find prepared dill dip, simply mix 1/2 cup plain yogurt or sour cream (or 1/4 cup each) with 2 teaspoons chopped fresh dill. Serve patties on a Kaiser roll or hamburger bun with lettuce, tomato slices and red onion slices if desired.

1 Serving: Calories 455 (Calories from Fat 205); Fat 23g (Saturated 10g); Cholesterol 190mg; Sodium 1400mg; Carbohydrate 32g (Dietary Fiber 2g); Protein 30g • **% Daily Value:** Vitamin A 16%; Vitamin C 4%; Calcium 38%; Iron 20% • **Exchanges:** 2 Starch, 3 Lean Meat, 3 Fat • **Carbohydrate Choices:** 2

Salmon Patties

Beer-Battered Fish

PREP: 8 MIN; COOK: 12 MIN

4 servings

Vegetable oil

1 pound fish fillets or 1 pound uncooked peeled deveined large shrimp, thawed if frozen

3 to 4 tablespoons Original Bisquick mix

1 cup Original Bisquick mix

1/2 cup regular or nonalcoholic beer

1/2 teaspoon salt

1 egg

Tartar sauce, if desired

1. Heat oil (1 1/2 inches) in heavy 3-quart saucepan or deep fryer to 350°. Lightly coat fish with 3 to 4 tablespoons Bisquick mix.

2. Beat 1 cup Bisquick mix, the beer, salt and egg with hand beater until smooth. (If batter is too thick, stir in additional beer, 1 tablespoon at a time, until desired consistency is reached.) Dip fish into batter, letting excess drip into bowl.

3. Fry fish in oil about 2 minutes on each side or until golden brown; drain. Serve hot with tartar sauce.

High Altitude (3500 to 6500 feet): Heat oil to 330° to 335°.

Betty's **TIP:** For a fish-fry experience at home, serve these crispy fish pieces in a plastic basket lined with cooking parchment or waxed paper. Add coleslaw, potato chips and tartar sauce. Or sandwich the fish in burger buns with tartar sauce, crisp lettuce leaves and a tomato slice for the Ultimate Fish Sandwich.

1 Serving: Calories 310 (Calories from Fat 110); Fat 12g (Saturated 3g); Cholesterol 115mg; Sodium 800mg; Carbohydrate 25g (Dietary Fiber 0g); Protein 25g • **% Daily Value:** Vitamin A 2%; Vitamin C 0%; Calcium 6%; Iron 6% • **Exchanges:** 1/2 Starch, 3 Lean Meat, 1 Fat • **Carbohydrate Choices:** 1 1/2

Beer-Battered Fish

Oven-Roasted Fish Dinner

PREP: 10 MIN; BAKE: 22 MIN

4 servings

1/2 cup Original or Reduced Fat
Bisquick mix

1/2 cup yellow cornmeal

1 teaspoon dried oregano leaves

1/2 teaspoon salt

1 to 1 1/2 pounds fish fillets

1/2 cup plain yogurt

1 medium zucchini, cut into 1-inch
pieces (1 1/2 cups)

1 medium red onion, cut into
wedges

1 medium red bell pepper,
cut into 8-inch pieces

1 tablespoon olive or vegetable oil

1. Heat oven to 450°. Spray jelly roll pan, 15 1/2 × 1 1/2 × 1 inch, with cooking spray.

2. Mix Bisquick mix, cornmeal, oregano and salt. Dip fish into yogurt, then coat with Bisquick mixture. Place in one side of pan. Toss remaining ingredients; spoon into other side of pan.

3. Bake uncovered 18 to 22 minutes or until vegetables are crisp-tender and fish flakes easily with fork.

High Altitude (3500 to 6500 feet): Bake 20 to 24 minutes.

Betty's **TIP:** For a citrusy flavor boost, sprinkle the fish with 1/2 teaspoon lemon pepper seasoning salt after baking and serve with lemon wedges. The next time you make this recipe, try a different mix of favorite vegetables such as eggplant, carrots and yellow summer squash.

1 Serving: Calories 270 (Calories from Fat 65); Fat 7g (Saturated 1g); Cholesterol 55mg; Sodium 620mg; Carbohydrate 31g (Dietary Fiber 3g); Protein 24g • **% Daily Value:** Vitamin A 44%; Vitamin C 52%; Calcium 10%; Iron 10% • **Exchanges:** 1 Starch, 3 Vegetable, 2 Lean Meat • **Carbohydrate Choices:** 2

Scrambled Eggs Alfredo Bake

PREP: 15 MIN; BAKE: 15 MIN

6 servings

1 cup Original Bisquick mix

6 tablespoons firm butter
  or margarine

1 egg

1/4 cup chopped onion

1/4 cup chopped green bell pepper

1 jar (4.5 ounces) sliced mushrooms,
  drained

12 eggs, beaten

1/3 cup crumbled cooked bacon

3/4 cup Alfredo pasta sauce

1. Heat oven to 400°. Spray bottom and sides of square baking dish, 8 × 8 × 2 inches, with cooking spray. Mix Bisquick mix and 4 tablespoons of the butter in small bowl with fork or pastry blender until crumbly. Gently stir in 1 egg; set aside.

2. Melt remaining 2 tablespoons butter in 12-inch nonstick skillet over medium heat. Cook onion, bell pepper and mushrooms in butter 3 to 5 minutes, stirring occasionally, until vegetables are crisp-tender. Add 12 beaten eggs to vegetable mixture. Cook, stirring occasionally, until eggs are set; remove from heat. Gently stir in bacon and pasta sauce. Spread in baking dish. Sprinkle Bisquick mixture over eggs.

3. Bake uncovered about 15 minutes until topping is golden brown.

High Altitude (3500 to 6500 feet): No changes.

Betty's **TIP:** Scrambled eggs for dinner? Why not! They're easy to make, kids love them, and with this combination of Alfredo sauce, bacon and vegetables, it's a hearty, savory meal sure to please the family whenever you decide to serve it.

1 Serving: Calories 485 (Calories from Fat 340); Fat 38g (Saturated 18g); Cholesterol 520mg; Sodium 770mg; Carbohydrate 17g (Dietary Fiber 1g); Protein 19g • **% Daily Value:** Vitamin A 28%; Vitamin C 4%; Calcium 18%; Iron 12% • **Exchanges:** 1 Starch, 2 1/2 High-Fat Meat, 3 Fat • **Carbohydrate Choices:** 1

Mexican Corn and Bean Cakes

PREP: 10 MIN; MICROWAVE: 6 MIN

6 servings

1 1/2 cups Original or Reduced
 Fat Bisquick mix

1/2 cup cornmeal

1 cup fat-free (skim) milk

3 egg whites

1 jar (16 ounces) thick 'n chunky
 salsa

1/2 cup canned whole kernel corn

2 tablespoons chopped ripe olives

1 cup fat-free refried beans
 (from 16-ounce can)

1/2 cup shredded reduced-fat
 Cheddar cheese (2 ounces)

1. Heat nonstick griddle to 375° or heat skillet over medium heat; grease with butter if necessary (or spray with cooking spray before heating). Stir Bisquick mix, cornmeal, milk and egg whites in large bowl until blended. Pour batter by 1/4 cupfuls onto hot griddle. Cook until edges are dry. Turn; cook other sides until golden.

2. Mix salsa, corn and olives. Place 1 corn cake on each of 6 micro-wavable serving plates; spread each cake with generous 2 table-spoons beans. Top each with additional corn cake. Spread 1/3 cup salsa mixture over top of each cake stack. Sprinkle each serving with generous 1 tablespoon cheese.

3. Microwave each serving uncovered on High about 1 minute or until heated through and cheese is melted. Serve with additional salsa and sour cream if desired.

High Altitude (3500 to 6500 feet): No changes.

Betty's **TIP:** Yellow cornmeal will give these corn cakes a buttery golden color, but white cornmeal will taste just as good, so use whatever you have on hand. For extra fiesta flavor, sprinkle with chopped fresh cilantro or place whole cilantro leaves on top of each stack.

1 Serving: Calories 275 (Calories from Fat 55); Fat 6g (Saturated 2g); Cholesterol 5mg; Sodium 1070mg; Carbohydrate 43g (Dietary Fiber 5g); Protein 12g • **% Daily Value:** Vitamin A 14%; Vitamin C 10%; Calcium 18%; Iron 16% • **Exchanges:** 3 Starch, 1/2 Lean Meat • **Carbohydrate Choices:** 3

Mexican Corn and Bean Cakes

Chapter 4

Impossibly Easy
PIES AND

Santa Fe Pizza (page 128) and Impossibly Easy Turkey Club Pie (page 138)

PIZZAS

Turkey Gyro Pizza

PREP: 15 MIN; BAKE: 25 MIN

6 servings

2 cups Original Bisquick mix

1/4 teaspoon dried oregano leaves

1/2 cup cold water

1/4 pound sliced deli turkey breast, cut into strips

1 can (2 1/4 ounces) sliced ripe olives, drained

1/2 cup crumbled feta cheese (2 ounces)

1 1/2 cups shredded mozzarella cheese (6 ounces)

1 small tomato, chopped (1/2 cup)

1/2 cup chopped cucumber

1. Move oven rack to lowest position. Heat oven to 425°. Spray 12-inch pizza pan with cooking spray. Stir Bisquick mix, oregano and water; beat vigorously with spoon 20 strokes until soft dough forms. Press dough in pizza pan, using fingers dipped in Bisquick mix; pinch edge to form 1/2-inch rim. Bake about 15 minutes or until golden brown.

2. Top crust with turkey and olives; sprinkle with feta and mozzarella cheeses.

3. Bake about 10 minutes or until cheese is melted. Sprinkle with tomato and cucumber.

High Altitude (3500 to 6500 feet): No changes.

Betty's **TIP:** The Mediterranean flavors and ingredients typical of a gyro—roasted meat with grilled vegetables and cucumber-yogurt sauce, rolled in pita bread—are transformed into a pizza the whole family will enjoy. If you prefer, mint leaves can be used in place of the oregano.

1 Serving: Calories 300 (Calories from Fat 125); Fat 14g (Saturated 7g); Cholesterol 35mg; Sodium 1180mg; Carbohydrate 28g (Dietary Fiber 1g); Protein 16g • **% Daily Value:** Vitamin A 8%; Vitamin C 6%; Calcium 34%; Iron 10% • **Exchanges:** 2 Starch, 1 1/2 Lean Meat, 1 Fat • **Carbohydrate Choices:** 2

Turkey Gyro Pizza

Fajita Pizza
PREP: 15 MIN; BAKE: 15 MIN

8 servings

2 tablespoons vegetable oil

1/2 pound boneless, skinless chicken breasts, cut into 1/8- to 1/4-inch strips

1/2 medium bell pepper, cut into thin strips

1 small onion, sliced

1/2 cup salsa or picante sauce

1 1/2 cups Original Bisquick mix

1/3 cup very hot water

1 1/2 cups shredded mozzarella cheese (6 ounces)

1. Move oven rack to lowest position. Heat oven to 450°. Spray 12-inch pizza pan with cooking spray. Heat 10-inch skillet over medium-high heat. Add oil; rotate skillet to coat bottom and side. Cook chicken in oil 3 minutes, stirring frequently. Stir in bell pepper and onion. Cook 3 to 4 minutes, stirring frequently, until vegetables are crisp-tender and chicken is no longer pink in center; remove from heat. Stir in salsa; set aside.

2. Stir Bisquick mix and very hot water until soft dough forms; beat vigorously with spoon 20 strokes. Press dough in pizza pan, using fingers dipped in Bisquick mix; pinch edge to form 1/2-inch rim.

3. Sprinkle 3/4 cup of the cheese over dough. Top with chicken mixture. Sprinkle with remaining 3/4 cup cheese. Bake 12 to 15 minutes or until crust is brown and cheese is melted and bubbly.

High Altitude (3500 to 6500 feet): Heat oven to 475°.

Betty's **TIP:** Keep your pizza crust crisp by sprinkling part of the cheese onto the unbaked pizza crust before topping with the moist sauce. The cheese forms a protective layer and helps prevent a soggy crust.

1 Serving: Calories 215 (Calories from Fat 100); Fat 11g (Saturated 4g); Cholesterol 30mg; Sodium 520mg; Carbohydrate 16g (Dietary Fiber 1g); Protein 14g • **% Daily Value:** Vitamin A 4%; Vitamin C 8%; Calcium 20%; Iron 6% • **Exchanges:** 1 Starch, 2 Lean Meat, 1 Fat • **Carbohydrate Choices:** 1

Fajita Pizza

Family-Favorite Cheese Pizza

PREP: 10 MIN; BAKE: 12 MIN; STAND: 2 MIN

8 servings

1 1/2 cups Original or Reduced
Fat Bisquick mix

1/3 cup very hot water

1/2 cup pizza sauce

1/2 teaspoon Italian seasoning

2 cups shredded mozzarella
cheese (8 ounces)

5 slices (3/4 ounce each) reduced-
fat process American cheese

1. Move oven rack to lowest position. Heat oven to 450°. Spray 12-inch pizza pan with cooking spray. Stir Bisquick mix and very hot water until soft dough forms; beat vigorously with spoon 20 strokes. Press dough in pizza pan, using fingers dipped in Bisquick mix; pinch edge to form 1/2-inch rim.

2. Spread pizza sauce over dough. Sprinkle with Italian seasoning and mozzarella cheese. Bake 10 to 12 minutes or until crust is golden and cheese is bubbly.

3. Cut American cheese into desired shapes with 2-inch cookie cutters. Arrange shapes on pizza. Let stand 1 to 2 minutes or until American cheese is melted.

High Altitude (3500 to 6500 feet): No changes.

Betty's **TIP:** In a hurry? Use preshredded cheese available in the dairy section of the supermarket. Be sure to use very hot water to make the pizza crust—it helps keep the crust from rising too high, and makes it chewy and crisp.

1 Serving: Calories 210 (Calories from Fat 90); Fat 10g (Saturated 5g); Cholesterol 20mg; Sodium 740mg; Carbohydrate 18g (Dietary Fiber 1g); Protein 12g • % **Daily Value:** Vitamin A 8%; Vitamin C 2%; Calcium 30%; Iron 4% • **Exchanges:** 1 Starch, 1 1/2 Medium-Fat Meat • **Carbohydrate Choices:** 1

Family-Favorite Cheese Pizza

Santa Fe Pizza

PREP: 15 MIN; BAKE: 28 MIN

Photo on page 120

8 servings

2 cups Original Bisquick mix

1/4 cup mild salsa-flavored or jalapeño-flavored process cheese sauce (room temperature)

1/4 cup hot water

1 can (16 ounces) refried beans

1/2 cup thick 'n chunky salsa

4 medium green onions, sliced (1/4 cup)

1 cup shredded Colby-Monterey Jack cheese (4 ounces)

1 cup shredded lettuce

1 medium tomato, chopped (3/4 cup)

1. Move oven rack to lowest position. Heat oven to 375°. Spray 12-inch pizza pan with cooking spray. Stir Bisquick mix, cheese sauce and hot water until soft dough forms; beat vigorously with spoon 20 strokes. Place dough on surface dusted with Bisquick mix; gently roll in Bisquick mix to coat. Shape into a ball; knead about 5 times or until smooth. Roll dough into 14-inch circle; place on cookie sheet.

2. Mix beans and salsa; spread over dough to within 2 inches of edge. Sprinkle with onions. Fold edge over bean mixture. Sprinkle cheese over bean mixture.

3. Bake 25 to 28 minutes or until crust is golden brown and cheese is melted. Garnish with lettuce and tomato.

High Altitude (3500 to 6500 feet): No changes.

Betty's **TIP:** If you're stopping at the grocery store, swing by the salad bar and pick up shredded lettuce, sliced green onions and chopped tomato to save prep time. Canned refried beans come in a variety of types—look for traditional, fat free or vegetarian.

1 Serving: Calories 260 (Calories from Fat 100); Fat 11g (Saturated 5g); Cholesterol 25mg; Sodium 800mg; Carbohydrate 30g (Dietary Fiber 4g); Protein 10g • **% Daily Value:** Vitamin A 10%; Vitamin C 8%; Calcium 18%; Iron 12% • **Exchanges:** 2 Starch, 1 High-Fat Meat • **Carbohydrate Choices:** 2

Sausage Pizza Pie

PREP: 15 MIN; BAKE: 25 MIN

8 servings

1 pound bulk pork sausage

1 can (8 ounces) pizza sauce

1/2 teaspoon dried oregano leaves

2 cups Original Bisquick mix

1/4 cup process cheese sauce (room temperature)

1/4 cup hot water

Green and red bell pepper rings, if desired

1 cup shredded mozzarella cheese (4 ounces)

1. Move oven rack to lowest position. Heat oven to 375°. Spray large cookie sheet with cooking spray. Cook sausage in 10-inch skillet over medium-high heat, stirring occasionally, until no longer pink; drain. Stir in pizza sauce and oregano; set aside.

2. Stir Bisquick mix, cheese sauce and hot water until soft dough forms. Place on surface dusted with Bisquick mix; roll in Bisquick mix to coat. Shape into a ball; knead 5 times. Roll into 14-inch circle; place on cookie sheet.

3. Spread sausage mixture over dough to within 3 inches of edge. Fold edge over mixture. Top with bell pepper rings. Sprinkle cheese over sausage mixture. Bake 23 to 25 minutes or until crust is light golden brown and cheese is melted.

High Altitude (3500 to 6500 feet): Heat oven to 400°.

Betty's **TIP:** Once you've rolled out the pizza dough, the easiest way to move it to the baking sheet is to fold the circle into quarters, then gently unfold onto the sheet.

1 Serving: Calories 280 (Calories from Fat 155); Fat 17g (Saturated 6g); Cholesterol 35mg; Sodium 110mg; Carbohydrate 22g (Dietary Fiber 1g); Protein 12g • **% Daily Value:** Vitamin A 6%; Vitamin C 6%; Calcium 22%; Iron 10% • **Exchanges:** 1 Starch, 1 Vegetable, 1 High-Fat Meat, 2 Fat • **Carbohydrate Choices:** 1 1/2

Salsa Pizza with Cheese Crust

PREP: 15 MIN; BAKE: 28 MIN

8 servings

1 pound ground beef

1 1/4 cups thick 'n chunky salsa

2 cups Original Bisquick mix

1/4 cup mild salsa-flavored or jalapeño-flavored process cheese sauce (room temperature)

1/4 cup hot water

4 medium green onions, sliced (1/4 cup)

1 cup shredded Colby-Monterey Jack cheese (4 ounces)

1. Move oven rack to lowest position. Heat oven to 375°. Spray 12-inch pizza pan with cooking spray. Cook beef in 10-inch skillet over medium heat, about 10 minutes, stirring occasionally, until brown; drain. Stir in salsa; remove from heat.

2. Stir Bisquick mix, cheese sauce and hot water until soft dough forms. Place dough on surface dusted with Bisquick mix; gently roll in Bisquick mix to coat. Shape into a ball; knead about 5 times or until smooth. Roll dough into 14-inch circle; place on cookie sheet.

3. Spread beef mixture over dough to within 2 inches of edge. Sprinkle with onions. Fold edge over beef mixture. Sprinkle cheese over beef mixture. Bake 25 to 28 minutes or until crust is golden brown and cheese is melted.

High Altitude (3500 to 6500 feet): No changes.

Betty's **TIP:** For a spicier crust, use the jalapeño-flavored cheese sauce. Garnish the pizza with chopped tomato, shredded lettuce, sliced ripe olives and pickled jalapeño slices for an extra kick.

1 Serving: Calories 310 (Calories from fat 160); Fat 18g (Saturated 8g); Cholesterol 50mg; Sodium 840mg; Carbohydrate 21g (Dietary Fiber 1g); Protein 17g • **% Daily Value:** Vitamin A 12%; Vitamin C 6%; Calcium 18%; Iron 14% • **Exchanges:** 1 Starch, 1 Vegetable, 2 High-Fat Meat • **Carbohydrate Choices:** 1 1/2

Salsa Pizza with Cheese Crust

Cheeseburger Pizza

PREP: 15 MIN; BAKE: 28 MIN; STAND: 5 MIN

8 servings

1 pound ground beef or ground turkey

1/2 cup process cheese sauce (room temperature)

2 cups Original Bisquick mix

1/4 cup process cheese sauce (room temperature)

1/4 cup hot water

1/4 cup shredded Colby-Monterey Jack cheese (1 ounce)

1 roma (plum) tomato, chopped (1/3 cup)

1. Move oven rack to lowest position. Heat oven to 375°. Spray 12-inch pizza pan with cooking spray. Cook beef in 10-inch skillet over medium-high heat, about 8 minutes, stirring occasionally, until brown; drain. Stir in 1/2 cup cheese sauce until cheese is melted.

2. Stir Bisquick mix, 1/4 cup cheese sauce and the hot water until soft dough forms; beat vigorously with spoon 20 strokes. Place dough on surface dusted with Bisquick mix; gently roll in Bisquick mix to coat. Shape into a ball; knead about 5 times or until smooth. Roll dough into 14-inch circle; place on cookie sheet.

3. Spoon beef mixture over dough to within 2 inches of edge. Fold edge over beef mixture. Bake 25 to 28 minutes or until crust is golden brown. Sprinkle with cheese and tomato. Let stand 5 minutes before cutting.

High Altitude (3500 to 6500 feet): No changes.

Betty's **TIP:** Make this family-favorite meal complete with carrot and celery sticks and frosty chocolate malts! Cheeseburger lovers may want to top this pizza with all their favorite fixin's—chopped onion, pickle relish, chopped tomato and even ketchup and mustard.

1 Serving: Calories 300 (Calories from Fat 155); Fat 17g (Saturated 7g); Cholesterol 45mg; Sodium 610mg; Carbohydrate 20g (Dietary Fiber 0g); Protein 16g • **% Daily Value:** Vitamin A 10%; Vitamin C 0%; Calcium 14%; Iron 10% • **Exchanges:** 1 Starch, 2 High-Fat Meat • **Carbohydrate Choices:** 1

Cheeseburger Pizza

Barbecued Beef and Cheese Pizza

PREP: 15 MIN; BAKE: 15 MIN

8 servings

1 pound ground beef

1 1/2 cups barbecue sauce

1 1/2 cups Original Bisquick mix

1/4 cup very hot water

1 tablespoon vegetable oil

Dill pickle slices, if desired

5 slices (1 ounce each) process American cheese, cut diagonally in half

1. Move oven rack to lowest position. Heat oven to 450°. Spray 12-inch pizza pan with cooking spray. Cook beef in 10-inch skillet over medium heat, about 10 minutes, stirring occasionally, until brown; drain. Stir in 1/2 cup of the barbecue sauce; set aside.

2. Stir Bisquick mix, very hot water and oil until dough forms; beat vigorously with spoon 20 strokes. Press dough in pizza pan, using fingers dipped in Bisquick mix; pinch edge to form 1/2-inch rim.

3. Spread remaining 1 cup barbecue sauce over dough. Top with beef mixture and pickle slices. Top with cheese. Bake 12 to 15 minutes or until crust is golden brown and cheese is melted.

High Altitude (3500 to 6500 feet): No changes.

Betty's **TIP:** After you grease the pizza pan, sprinkle it with cornmeal for added crust crispness. One pound of bulk pork sausage makes a tasty variation in place of the ground beef.

1 Serving: Calories 330 (Calories from Fat 150); Fat 17g (Saturated 7g); Cholesterol 45mg; Sodium 1000mg; Carbohydrate 30g (Dietary Fiber 0g); Protein 15g • **% Daily Value:** Vitamin A 6%; Vitamin C 0%; Calcium 12%; Iron 12% • **Exchanges:** 2 Starch, 2 High-Fat Meat, 1/2 Fat • **Carbohydrate Choices:** 2

Hot Sub Deep-Dish Pizza

PREP: 15 MIN; BAKE: 20 MIN

8 servings

3 cups Original or Reduced Fat Bisquick mix

2/3 cup very hot water

2 tablespoons vegetable oil

1 1/4 cups pizza or spaghetti sauce

8 to 10 thin slices assorted deli or luncheon meats

1 large green bell pepper, thinly sliced into rings

2 tablespoons Italian dressing

6 slices (1 ounce each) Cheddar cheese, cut diagonally in half

1. Move oven rack to lowest position. Heat oven to 425°. Spray bottom and sides of jelly roll pan, 15 1/2 × 10 1/2 × 1 inch, or cookie sheet with cooking spray.

2. Stir Bisquick mix, very hot water and oil until dough forms; beat vigorously with spoon 20 strokes. Pat or press dough in bottom and up sides of pan, using hands dipped in Bisquick mix. Or pat dough into 13 × 10-inch rectangle on cookie sheet; pinch edges, forming 3/4-inch rim.

3. Spread pizza sauce over dough. Top with meats and bell pepper. Drizzle with dressing. Top with cheese. Bake 15 to 20 minutes or until crust is golden brown and cheese is melted and bubbly.

High Altitude (3500 to 6500 feet): Bake 17 to 20 minutes.

Betty's **TIP:** To reduce the fat to 10 grams and the calories to 280 per serving, use Reduced Fat Bisquick mix, fat-free Italian dressing and reduced-fat Cheddar cheese. Any combination of ham, turkey, large slices of pepperoni, salami, bologna or other cold cuts will work in this recipe. The possibilities are endless!

1 Serving: Calories 390 (Calories from Fat 190); Fat 21g (Saturated 7g); Cholesterol 30mg; Sodium 1220mg; Carbohydrate 37g (Dietary Fiber 1g); Protein 12g • **% Daily Value:** Vitamin A 10%; Vitamin C 20%; Calcium 20%; Iron 12% • **Exchanges:** 2 1/2 Starch, 1 High-Fat Meat, 2 Fat • **Carbohydrate Choices:** 2 1/2

kids LOVE

Pizza Pot Pies
PREP: 20 MIN; BAKE: 20 MIN

5 servings

1 pound ground beef

1 medium onion, chopped (1/2 cup)

1 small green bell pepper, chopped (1/2 cup)

1 can (8 ounces) pizza sauce

1 can (4 ounces) mushroom pieces and stems, drained

1 cup shredded mozzarella cheese (4 ounces)

1 cup Original Bisquick mix

1/4 cup boiling water

1. Heat oven to 375°. Spray bottom and sides of five 10- to 12-ounce casseroles with cooking spray. Cook beef, onion and bell pepper in 10-inch skillet over medium heat, about 10 minutes, stirring occasionally, until beef is brown; drain.

2. Stir pizza sauce and mushrooms into beef. Heat to boiling; reduce heat. Simmer uncovered 5 minutes, stirring occasionally. Spoon beef mixture into casseroles. Sprinkle 1/4 cup of the cheese on each.

3. Stir Bisquick mix and boiling water until soft dough forms; beat vigorously with spoon 20 strokes. Place dough on surface dusted with Bisquick mix; gently roll in Bisquick mix to coat. Shape into a ball; knead about 10 times or until smooth. Divide dough into 5 balls. Pat each ball into a circle the size of casserole diameter. Place each circle on beef mixture in casserole.

4. Bake 15 to 20 minutes or until crust is very light brown.

High Altitude (3500 to 6500 feet): Bake 22 to 25 minutes.

Betty's **TIP:** For variety, add sliced olives, chopped tomatoes or sliced pepperoni, cut into fourths, to the pizza sauce mixture. For a special occasion, use a small cookie cutter to cut a jack-o'-lantern, cat, pumpkin or moon shape out of the dough circle before putting it on the beef mixture.

1 Serving: Calories 395 (Calories from Fat 200); Fat 22g (Saturated 9g); Cholesterol 65mg; Sodium 810mg; Carbohydrate 23g (Dietary Fiber 2g); Protein 26g • **% Daily Value:** Vitamin A 10%; Vitamin C 20%; Calcium 284; Iron 16% • **Exchanges:** 1 Starch, 1 Vegetable, 3 Medium-Fat Meat, 1 1/2 Fat • **Carbohydrate Choices:** 1 1/2

Pizza Pot Pies

Impossibly Easy Turkey Club Pie

PREP: 14 MIN; BAKE: 35 MIN; STAND: 5 MIN

Photo on page 121

6 servings

1 1/2 cups cut-up cooked turkey

8 slices bacon, crisply cooked and crumbled

1 cup shredded Cheddar cheese (4 ounces)

1/2 cup Original or Reduced Fat Bisquick mix

1 cup milk

2 eggs

1. Heat oven to 400°. Spray bottom and side of pie plate, 9 × 1 1/4 inches, with cooking spray. Sprinkle turkey, bacon and cheese in pie plate.

2. Stir remaining ingredients until blended. Pour into pie plate.

3. Bake 30 to 35 minutes or until knife inserted in center comes out clean. Let stand 5 minutes before serving.

High Altitude (3500 to 6500 feet): No changes.

Betty's **TIP:** Get a head start on your dinner by cooking the bacon, cutting up the turkey and shredding the cheese the night before. Enjoy an easy one-dish meal by topping the pie with shredded lettuce and sliced tomatoes. For dessert, serve fruit-yogurt smoothies.

1 Serving: Calories 275 (Calories from Fat 155); Fat 17g (Saturated 8g); Cholesterol 130mg; Sodium 460mg; Carbohydrate 8g (Dietary Fiber 0g); Protein 21g • **% Daily Value:** Vitamin A 8%; Vitamin C 0%; Calcium 18%; Iron 6% • **Exchanges:** 1/2 Starch, 3 Medium-Fat Meat • **Carbohydrate Choices:** 1/2

Impossibly Easy Oktoberfest Pie

PREP: 10 MIN; BAKE: 35 MIN; STAND: 5 MIN

6 servings

1/2 pound fully cooked bratwurst (about 3), cut into 3/4-inch pieces

1 can (8 ounces) sauerkraut, drained (1 1/3 cups)

1 cup shredded Swiss cheese (4 ounces)

3/4 cup Original or Reduced Fat Bisquick mix

1/2 cup milk

1/2 cup regular or nonalcoholic beer

2 eggs

1. Heat oven to 400°. Spray bottom and side of pie plate, 9 × 1 1/4 inches, with cooking spray. Sprinkle bratwurst, sauerkraut and cheese in pie plate.

2. Stir remaining ingredients until blended. Pour into pie plate.

3. Bake 30 to 35 minutes or until knife inserted in center comes out clean. Let stand 5 minutes before serving.

High Altitude (3500 to 6500 feet): No changes.

Betty's **TIP:** Pie plates vary in size—and using too small a pan will cause the filling to run over while baking. Pie plate sizes are usually marked on the backs of the plates; if not marked, measure from inside rim to inside rim. Serve this pie with sliced apples on a bed of greens drizzled with poppy seed dressing and rye rolls or bread.

1 Serving: Calories 285 (Calories from Fat 180); Fat 20g (Saturated 8g); Cholesterol 110mg; Sodium 930mg; Carbohydrate 15g (Dietary Fiber 1g); Protein 14g • **% Daily Value:** Vitamin A 6%; Vitamin C 4%; Calcium 24%; Iron 8% • **Exchanges:** 1/2 Starch, 1 Vegetable, 2 Medium-Fat Meat, 2 Fat • **Carbohydrate Choices:** 1

kids LOVE

Impossibly Easy Calico Corn and Bacon Pie

PREP: 15 MIN; BAKE: 30 MIN; STAND: 5 MIN

6 servings

8 slices bacon, crisply cooked and crumbled (1/2 cup)

1 small onion, chopped (1/4 cup)

1/4 cup chopped green bell pepper

1 can (about 8 ounces) whole kernel corn, drained

1 jar (2 ounces) diced pimientos, drained

2/3 cup Original or Reduced Fat Bisquick mix

1 cup milk

1/8 teaspoon pepper

2 eggs

Sour cream, if desired

1. Heat oven to 400°. Spray bottom and side of pie plate, 9 × 1 1/4 inches, with cooking spray. Reserve 2 tablespoons of the bacon. Sprinkle remaining bacon, the onion, bell pepper, corn and pimientos in pie plate.

2. Stir remaining ingredients, except sour cream, until blended. Pour into pie plate.

3. Bake uncovered about 30 minutes or until knife inserted in center comes out clean. Let stand 5 minutes before serving. Garnish with sour cream and reserved bacon.

High Altitude (3500 to 6500 feet): No changes.

Betty's **TIP:** Get a jump start on dinner. Mix up this tasty pie the night or morning before, then pop it in the oven when you get home from work! After adding all ingredients to pie plate, cover and refrigerate up to 24 hours. Uncover and bake 30 to 35 minutes (33 to 38 minutes at high altitude).

1 Serving: Calories 185 (Calories from Fat 80); Fat 9g (Saturated 3g); Cholesterol 80mg; Sodium 440mg; Carbohydrate 18g (Dietary Fiber 1g, Sugars 5g); Protein 8g • **% Daily Value:** Vitamin A 10%; Vitamin C 14%; Calcium 8%; Iron 6% • **Exchanges:** 1 Starch, 1 Vegetable, 1/2 High-Fat Meat, 1 Fat • **Carbohydrate Choices:** 1

Impossibly Easy Calico Corn and Bacon Pie

Impossibly Easy Vegetable Pie

PREP: 15 MIN; BAKE: 35 MIN; STAND: 5 MIN

6 servings

2 cups chopped broccoli or sliced cauliflowerets

1/3 cup chopped onion

1/3 cup chopped green bell pepper

1 cup shredded Cheddar cheese (4 ounces)

1/2 cup Original Bisquick mix

1 cup milk

1/2 teaspoon salt

1/4 teaspoon pepper

2 eggs

1. Heat oven to 400°. Spray bottom and side of pie plate, 9 × 1 1/4 inches, with cooking spray. Heat 1 inch water (salted if desired) to boiling in 2-quart saucepan. Add broccoli; cover and heat to boiling. Cook about 5 minutes or until almost tender; drain thoroughly.

2. Mix broccoli, onion, bell pepper and cheese in pie plate. Stir remaining ingredients until blended. Pour into pie plate.

3. Bake uncovered 30 to 35 minutes or until golden brown and knife inserted in center comes out clean. Let stand 5 minutes before cutting.

High Altitude (3500 to 6500 feet): Heat oven to 425°. Bake about 30 minutes.

Betty's **TIP:** Use a 9-ounce package of cut broccoli from the freezer instead of the fresh broccoli. Thaw, drain and add to the pie. For Impossibly Easy Spinach Pie, use a 9-ounce package of frozen spinach, thawed and squeezed to drain, in place of the broccoli; do not cook. Omit bell pepper. Substitute Swiss cheese for the Cheddar cheese. Add 1/4 teaspoon ground nutmeg with the pepper. Bake about 30 minutes.

1 Serving: Calories 170 (Calories from Fat 90); Fat 10g (Saturated 5g); Cholesterol 95mg; Sodium 500mg; Carbohydrate 11g (Dietary Fiber 1g); Protein 10g • **% Daily Value:** Vitamin A 16%; Vitamin C 14%; Calcium 18%; Iron 4% • **Exchanges:** 1/2 Starch, 1 Vegetable, 1 Medium-Fat Meat, 1 Fat • **Carbohydrate Choices:** 1

Impossibly Easy Vegetable Pie

Impossibly Easy Quesadilla Pie

PREP: 8 MIN; BAKE: 30 MIN; STAND: 5 MIN

6 servings

1 can (4 ounces) chopped green chiles, well drained

2 cups shredded Cheddar cheese (8 ounces)

1 teaspoon chopped fresh cilantro or parsley

3/4 cup Original or Reduced Fat Bisquick mix

1 1/2 cups milk

3 eggs

Salsa, if desired

1. Heat oven to 400°. Spray bottom and side of pie plate, 9 × 1 1/4 inches, with cooking spray. Sprinkle chilies, cheese and cilantro in pie plate.

2. Stir Bisquick mix, milk and eggs until blended. Pour into pie plate.

3. Bake 25 to 30 minutes or until knife inserted in center comes out clean. Let stand 5 minutes before serving. Serve with salsa.

High Altitude (3500 to 6500 feet): Use 1 1/4 cups milk. Bake 30 to 35 minutes.

Betty's **TIP:** You can also use Monterey Jack cheese, or for some extra heat, use Monterey Jack cheese with jalapeño peppers. This zesty pie is great topped with shredded lettuce, chopped tomatoes and green onions.

1 Serving: Calories 280 (Calories from Fat 160); Fat 18g (Saturated 10g); Cholesterol 115mg; Sodium 580mg; Carbohydrate 14g (Dietary Fiber 0g); Protein 16g • **% Daily Value:** Vitamin A 16%; Vitamin C 6%; Calcium 32%; Iron 6% • **Exchanges:** 1/2 Milk, 1 Vegetable, 1 High-Fat Meat, 2 Fat • **Carbohydrate Choices:** 1

Impossibly Easy Seafood Pie

PREP: 15 MIN; BAKE: 40 MIN; STAND: 5 MIN

6 servings

1 package (6 ounces) frozen ready-to-serve crabmeat, thawed and drained

1 cup shredded sharp Cheddar cheese (4 ounces)

1 package (3 ounces) cream cheese, cut into 1/4-inch cubes and softened

4 medium green onions, sliced (1/4 cup)

1 jar (2 ounces) diced pimientos, drained, if desired

1/2 cup Original or Reduced Fat Bisquick mix

1 cup milk

1/2 teaspoon salt

2 eggs

1. Heat oven to 400°. Spray bottom and side of pie plate, 9 × 1 1/4 inches, with cooking spray. Mix crabmeat, cheeses, onions and pimientos in pie plate.

2. Stir remaining ingredients until blended. Pour into pie plate.

3. Bake 35 to 40 minutes or until golden brown and knife inserted in center comes out clean (some cream cheese may stick to knife). Let stand 5 minutes before serving.

High Altitude (3500 to 6500 feet): No changes.

Betty's **TIP:** Try 1 package (4 ounces) frozen cooked salad shrimp, thawed, or 1 can (4 to 4 1/2 ounces) shrimp, rinsed and drained, instead of the crabmeat. Or use 1 can (6 ounces) tuna, drained. Cover and refrigerate any leftover Impossibly Easy Pie up to 24 hours. To reheat a slice, cover and microwave on Medium (50%) 2 to 3 minutes or until hot. Let stand 2 minutes before serving.

1 Serving: Calories 230 (Calories from Fat 135); Fat 15g (Saturated 9g); Cholesterol 145mg; Sodium 620mg; Carbohydrate 10g (Dietary Fiber 0g); Protein 14g • **% Daily Value:** Vitamin A 18%; Vitamin C 8%; Calcium 22%; Iron 8% • **Exchanges:** 1 Starch, 2 Lean Meat, 1 Fat • **Carbohydrate Choices:** 1

Impossibly Easy Salmon-Asparagus Bake

PREP: 15 MIN; BAKE: 45 MIN; STAND: 5 MIN

12 to 16 servings

2 packages (10 ounces each)
   frozen cut asparagus, thawed
   and well drained

8 medium green onions, sliced
   (1/2 cup)

3 cups shredded Swiss cheese
   (12 ounces)

2 cans (6 to 7 1/2 ounces each)
   salmon or tuna, drained and
   flaked

1 1/2 cups Original or Reduced
   Fat Bisquick mix

1 1/2 cups milk

1 tablespoon chopped fresh or
   1 teaspoon dried basil leaves

1/4 teaspoon pepper

4 eggs

1. Heat oven to 400°. Spray rectangular baking dish, 13 × 9 × 2 inches, with cooking spray. Sprinkle asparagus, onions, 1 1/2 cups of the cheese and the salmon in baking dish.

2. Stir remaining ingredients, except cheese, until blended. Pour into baking dish.

3. Bake 40 to 45 minutes or until knife inserted in center comes out clean. Sprinkle with remaining 1 1/2 cups cheese. Bake about 2 minutes or until cheese is melted. Let stand 5 minutes before serving.

High Altitude (3500 to 6500 feet): No changes.

Betty's **TIP:** You can prepare this dish ahead of time. Just cover the assembled dish and refrigerate overnight. To serve, uncover and bake 50 to 55 minutes for a complete-with-vegetable homemade dinner.

1 Serving: Calories 255 (Calories from Fat 120); Fat 14g (Saturated 7g); Cholesterol 110mg; Sodium 420mg; Carbohydrate 14g (Dietary Fiber 1g); Protein 19g • **% Daily Value:** Vitamin A 16%; Vitamin C 10%; Calcium 42%; Iron 8% • **Exchanges:** 1 Starch, 2 Medium-Fat Meat, 1/2 Fat • **Carbohydrate Choices:** 1

Impossibly Easy Salmon-Asparagus Bake

kids LOVE

Impossibly Easy Triple-Cheese Pie

PREP: 10 MIN; BAKE: 45 MIN; STAND: 5 MIN

6 servings

1 cup small curd creamed cottage cheese

1 cup shredded mozzarella cheese (4 ounces)

1 cup shredded Cheddar cheese (4 ounces)

1/2 cup chopped bell pepper

1 cup Original Bisquick mix

1 1/2 cups milk

4 eggs

3/4 cup canned French-fried onions

1. Heat oven to 400°. Spray bottom and side of pie plate, 10 × 1 1/2 inches, with cooking spray. Mix cheeses and bell pepper; spread in pie plate.

2. Stir Bisquick mix, milk and eggs until blended. Pour into pie plate. Sprinkle with onions.

3. Bake 40 to 45 minutes or until golden brown and knife inserted in center comes out clean. Let stand 5 minutes before serving.

High Altitude (3500 to 6500 feet): No changes.

Betty's **TIP:** Get the whole family involved! Making a meal together allows you to spend time with your children. Let young children set the table, wash vegetables and load the dishwasher. Older children can shred cheese and help assemble recipes. What kid wouldn't be proud of helping to make this main-dish pie!

1 Serving: Calories 370 (Calories from Fat 200); Fat 22g (Saturated 10g); Cholesterol 180mg; Sodium 770mg; Carbohydrate 21g (Dietary Fiber 1g); Protein 22g • **% Daily Value:** Vitamin A 14%; Vitamin C 8%; Calcium 38%; Iron 8% • **Exchanges:** 1 Starch, 1/2 Milk, 2 Medium-Fat Meat, 2 Fat • **Carbohydrate Choices:** 1 1/2

Impossibly Easy Triple-Cheese Pie

Chapter 5

Feed a CROWD

Baked Taco Sandwich (page 160), Cheese-Garlic Biscuits (page 173) and Sausage Casserole with Cheesy Corn Bread (page 161)

kids LOVE

Layered Biscuit Chicken Divan

PREP: 15 MIN; BAKE: 35 MIN

10 servings

1 package (9 ounces) frozen chicken breast strips, thawed and cut in half if necessary

1 jar (1 pound) roasted garlic Parmesan pasta sauce (white sauce)

1 bag (1 pound) frozen broccoli cuts, thawed, drained and patted dry

2 cups Original Bisquick mix

1 cup milk

1/2 cup sour cream

1/4 cup grated Parmesan cheese

1. Heat oven to 375°. Heat chicken, pasta sauce and broccoli to boiling in 3-quart saucepan, stirring frequently. Spread half of the mixture in ungreased square pan, 9 × 9 × 2 inches.

2. Stir Bisquick mix, milk and sour cream until blended. Pour half of the batter over chicken mixture in pan. Spread with remaining chicken mixture; top with remaining batter. Sprinkle with cheese.

3. Bake uncovered about 35 minutes or until toothpick inserted in center comes out clean.

High Altitude (3500 to 6500 feet): Bake about 40 minutes.

Betty's **TIP:** Create fun family moments by letting the kids help with dinner; they can stir the Bisquick mixture and sprinkle cheese over the top. While you're waiting for dinner to bake, have them set the table and help you mix up a quick salad. Serve dinner with Cheddar and Green Onion Biscuit Poppers, page 70, or Cheddar–Green Olive Breadsticks, page 65.

1 Serving: Calories 250 (Calories from Fat 90); Fat 10g (Saturated 4g); Cholesterol 30mg; Sodium 510mg; Carbohydrate 27g (Dietary Fiber 2g); Protein 13g · **% Daily Value:** Vitamin A 18%; Vitamin C 14%; Calcium 16%; Iron 8% · **Exchanges:** 1 1/2 Starch, 1 Vegetable, 1 Medium-Fat Meat, 1 Fat · **Carbohydrate Choices:** 2

Layered Biscuit Chicken Divan

ULTIMATE Oven-Fried Chicken

PREP: 10 MIN; STAND: 5 MIN; BAKE: 50 MIN

12 servings

1 cup buttermilk

12 boneless, skinless chicken breast halves (3 3/4 pounds)

1 1/2 cups cornflakes cereal

1 1/2 cups Original Bisquick mix

2 envelopes (1 ounce each) ranch dressing mix

Cooking spray

1. Heat oven to 400°. Spray jelly roll pan, 15 1/2 × 10 1/2 × 1 inch, with cooking spray; set aside. Pour buttermilk into rectangular baking dish, 13 × 9 × 2 inches. Add chicken; turn to coat. Let stand 5 minutes.

2. Divide cereal between two 1-gallon resealable plastic food-storage bags, placing 3/4 cup cereal in each bag; crush with rolling pin. Add 3/4 cup of the Bisquick mix and 1 envelope dressing mix (dry) to cereal in each bag. Remove chicken from buttermilk; discard buttermilk. Add a few pieces of chicken at a time to cereal mixture. Seal bag; shake to coat.

3. Place chicken in jelly roll pan. Spray with cooking spray. Bake uncovered 40 to 50 minutes or until juice of chicken is no longer pink when centers of thickest pieces are cut.

High Altitude (3500 to 6500 feet): No changes.

Betty's **TIP:** Did you know that buttermilk, with its thick consistency and slightly tangy flavor, has long been a cook's "secret" for making fried chicken? You can enjoy this chicken hot or cold—if you'd like to make and take, bake it the night before, and then pack it up for a picnic in the park the next day!

1 Serving: Calories 230 (Calories from Fat 55); Fat 6g (Saturated 2g); Cholesterol 75mg; Sodium 680mg; Carbohydrate 16g (Dietary Fiber 0g); Protein 29g • % **Daily Value:** Vitamin A 2%; Vitamin C 2%; Calcium 8%; Iron 14% • **Exchanges:** 1 Starch, 4 Very Lean Meat • **Carbohydrate Choices:** 1

Ultimate Oven-Fried Chicken

Quick Cheeseburger and Vegetable Bake

PREP: 14 MIN; BAKE: 35 MIN

16 to 20 servings

1 1/2 pounds ground beef

1 1/4 cups chopped onions (about 2 large)

1 can (10 3/4 ounces) condensed Cheddar cheese soup

1 1/4 cups frozen mixed vegetables (from 1-pound bag), if desired

1/2 cup milk

2 1/3 cups Original Bisquick mix

2/3 cup water

1 1/3 cups shredded Cheddar cheese (about 5 ounces)

1. Heat oven to 375°. Generously spray bottom and sides of jelly roll pan, 15 1/2 × 10 1/2 × 1 inch, with cooking spray. Cook beef and onions in 12-inch skillet over medium heat, about 10 minutes, stirring occasionally, until beef is brown; drain. Stir in soup, vegetables and milk.

2. Stir Bisquick mix and water until moistened. Spread evenly in pan. Spread beef mixture over batter. Sprinkle with cheese.

3. Bake uncovered 35 minutes.

High Altitude (3500 to 6500 feet): Do not add cheese before baking. Bake 35 minutes. Sprinkle with cheese. Bake about 5 minutes longer or until cheese is melted.

Betty's **TIP:** Mushroom-lovers can use 1 1/2 cups of sliced fresh mushrooms in place of the onions. For an easy meal with lots of crowd appeal, put together a fresh-vegetable tray and a purchased dip while this recipe is in the oven. For dessert, top brownie squares with butter pecan or butter brickle ice cream and drizzle with chocolate sauce.

1 Serving: Calories 225 (Calories from Fat 115); Fat 13g (Saturated 6g); Cholesterol 35mg; Sodium 500mg; Carbohydrate 14g (Dietary Fiber 0g); Protein 13g • **% Daily Value:** Vitamin A 10%; Vitamin C 0%; Calcium 10%; Iron 8% • **Exchanges:** 1 Starch, 1 1/2 High-Fat Meat • **Carbohydrate Choices:** 1

Quick Cheeseburger and Vegetable Bake

Easy Sloppy Joe Bake

PREP: 15 MIN; BAKE: 30 MIN

12 servings

2 pounds ground beef

2 medium onions, chopped
  (1 cup)

2 cans (15.5 ounces each) original
  sloppy joe sauce

2 cups shredded Cheddar cheese
  (8 ounces)

2 cups Original Bisquick mix

1 cup milk

2 eggs

1. Heat oven to 400°. Cook beef and onions in ovenproof 12-inch skillet over medium heat, about 10 minutes, stirring occasionally, until beef is brown; drain. Stir in sloppy joe sauce. Sprinkle with cheese.

2. Stir remaining ingredients until blended. Pour over beef mixture. If skillet is not ovenproof, cover handle with aluminum foil.

3. Bake uncovered about 30 minutes or until golden brown.

High Altitude (3500 to 6500 feet): Cook beef and onions over medium-high heat.

Betty's **TIP:** For a change of pace, use 2 pounds of ground chicken or turkey instead of the ground beef. As a time-saver, use 1 cup frozen chopped onion or 1/4 cup instant minced onion instead of the fresh onion, then garnish this easy supper with slices of crisp, juicy apples.

1 Serving: Calories 420 (Calories from Fat 190); Fat 21g (Saturated 9g); Cholesterol 100mg; Sodium 1500mg; Carbohydrate 35g (Dietary Fiber 2g); Protein 23g • **% Daily Value:** Vitamin A 28%; Vitamin C 12%; Calcium 18%; Iron 14% • **Exchanges:** 2 Starch, 2 1/2 Medium-Fat Meat, 1/2 Fat • **Carbohydrate Choices:** 2

Easy Sloppy Joe Bake

Baked Taco Sandwich

PREP: 12 MIN; BAKE: 30 MIN; STAND: 2 MIN

Photo on page 150

16 to 20 servings

2 pounds ground beef

2 envelopes (1.25 ounces each)
  taco seasoning mix

2 cups Original Bisquick mix

2/3 cup cold water

2 cups shredded Cheddar cheese
  (8 ounces)

1. Heat oven to 450°. Spray bottom and sides of jelly roll pan, 15 1/2 × 10 1/2 × 1 inch, with cooking spray. Cook beef and seasoning mix as directed on envelope of seasoning mix.

2. Stir Bisquick mix and water until soft dough forms; spread in pan. Spread beef mixture over dough.

3. Bake uncovered 25 to 30 minutes or until edges are golden brown and toothpick inserted in center comes out clean. Immediately sprinkle with cheese. Let stand 1 to 2 minutes or until cheese is melted.

High Altitude (3500 to 6500 feet): No changes.

Betty's **TIP:** To add flavor and color, stir two 15.25-ounce cans of drained whole kernel corn into the cooked beef mixture before spreading it in the pan. Make a taco buffet—set out colorful bowls filled with shredded cheese, guacamole, chopped tomatoes, torn lettuce, sliced ripe olives, sour cream and salsa.

1 Serving: Calories 240 (Calories from Fat 135); Fat 15g (Saturated 7g); Cholesterol 45mg; Sodium 510mg; Carbohydrate 12g (Dietary Fiber 1g); Protein 15g • **% Daily Value:** Vitamin A 12%; Vitamin C 0%; Calcium 12%; Iron 8% • **Exchanges:** 1 Starch, 2 Medium-Fat Meat • **Carbohydrate Choices:** 1

Sausage Casserole with Cheesy Corn Bread

PREP: 10 MIN; BAKE: 32 MIN

Photo on page 151

10 servings

1 ring (1 pound) fully cooked smoked sausage or kielbasa, cut into 1/4-inch slices

1 bag (1 pound) frozen broccoli, carrots and cauliflower, thawed and drained

2 cans (10 3/4 ounces each) condensed Cheddar cheese soup

1 1/4 cups Original Bisquick mix

1 1/2 cups milk

3/4 cup cornmeal

2 eggs

1 cup shredded Cheddar cheese (4 ounces)

1. Heat oven to 450°. Spray bottom and sides of rectangular pan, 13 × 9 × 2 inches, with cooking spray. Mix sausage, vegetables and soup in pan.

2. Stir Bisquick mix, milk, cornmeal, eggs and 1/2 cup of the cheese until blended. Pour over sausage mixture.

3. Bake uncovered 25 to 30 minutes; sprinkle with remaining 1/2 cup cheese and continue to bake 1 or 2 minutes more, until light brown.

High Altitude (3500 to 6500 feet): Bake about 30 minutes.

Betty's **TIP:** Check out your freezer and pantry—you can use a 1-pound bag of frozen mixed vegetables or an equal amount of any of your favorite frozen vegetable combinations (thawed and drained) in this casserole. You can also substitute condensed nacho cheese soup or a 16-ounce jar of double Cheddar cheese pasta sauce for the Cheddar cheese soup.

1 Serving: Calories 400 (Calories from Fat 225); Fat 25g (Saturated 11g); Cholesterol 95mg; Sodium 1340mg; Carbohydrate 28g (Dietary Fiber 2g); Protein 16g • **% Daily Value:** Vitamin A 94%; Vitamin C 8%; Calcium 20%; Iron 10% • **Exchanges:** 2 Starch, 1 1/2 High-Fat Meat, 2 Fat • **Carbohydrate Choices:** 2

Roast Beef Pot Pie

PREP: 15 MIN; BAKE: 30 MIN

12 servings

2 cups cubed cooked roast beef

2 jars (12 ounces each) beef gravy

2 bags (1 pound each) frozen potatoes, carrots, celery and onions

1 teaspoon seasoned salt

2 cups Original Bisquick mix

1 1/2 cups milk

1. Heat oven to 400°. Heat beef, gravy, frozen vegetables and seasoned salt to boiling in 4-quart Dutch oven, stirring constantly. Boil and stir 1 minute. Spread in ungreased 3-quart casserole.

2. Stir Bisquick mix and milk until blended. Pour evenly over beef mixture.

3. Bake uncovered about 30 minutes or until light brown.

High Altitude (3500 to 6500 feet): Bake uncovered about 35 minutes.

Betty's **TIP:** Love herbs? Add extra flavor to the topping by stirring in either 1 teaspoon Italian seasoning, 1 teaspoon dried dill weed or 1/2 teaspoon garlic or onion powder with the Bisquick mix. At Thanksgiving, turn leftovers into Turkey Pot Pie by using 2 cups cubed roasted turkey and leftover gravy or jarred chicken gravy instead of the roast beef and beef gravy.

1 Serving: Calories 215 (Calories from Fat 70); Fat 8g (Saturated 3g); Cholesterol 20mg; Sodium 860mg; Carbohydrate 25g (Dietary Fiber 2g); Protein 11g • **% Daily Value:** Vitamin A 78%; Vitamin C 2%; Calcium 8%; Iron 10% • **Exchanges:** 1 1/2 Starch, 1 High-Fat Meat • **Carbohydrate Choices:** 1 1/2

Roast Beef Pot Pie

Vegetable-Cheese Strata

PREP: 13 MIN; COOL: 45 MIN; CHILL: 2 HR; BAKE: 1 HR 28 MIN; STAND: 10 MIN

8 servings

1 2/3 cups Original Bisquick mix

3 tablespoons Italian dressing

3 tablespoons milk

1 bag (1 pound) frozen broccoli, green beans, pearl onions and red peppers (or other combination), thawed and drained

3 cups milk

1 teaspoon yellow mustard

1/2 teaspoon seasoned salt

1/4 teaspoon pepper

8 eggs

2 cups shredded Cheddar cheese (8 ounces)

1. Heat oven to 450°. Generously spray bottom and sides of rectangular baking dish, 13 × 9 × 2 inches, with cooking spray. Stir Bisquick mix, Italian dressing and 3 tablespoons milk in medium bowl until soft dough forms. Pat dough on bottom of baking dish. Bake 8 minutes. Cool completely, about 45 minutes.

2. Sprinkle vegetables over baked crust. Beat remaining ingredients except cheese in medium bowl with wire whisk or fork until blended. Pour over vegetables. Sprinkle with cheese. Cover and refrigerate at least 2 hours.

3. Heat oven to 350°. Cover and bake 30 minutes. Uncover and bake 40 to 50 minutes longer or until knife inserted in center comes out clean. Let stand 10 minutes before cutting.

High Altitude (3500 to 6500 feet): Bake crust in step 1 for 12 minutes.

Betty's **TIP:** You can make this easy strata on your schedule so it's ready when you are. It can be refrigerated up to 24 hours before baking and will still bake in about the same amount of time. That makes it a great choice for an easy brunch or potluck dinner. For meat-lovers, serve Canadian-style bacon, bacon strips or sausage on the side.

1 Serving: Calories 365 (Calories from Fat 200); Fat 22g (Saturated 10g); Cholesterol 250mg; Sodium 790mg; Carbohydrate 25g (Dietary Fiber 2g); Protein 19g • **% Daily Value:** Vitamin A 38%; Vitamin C 28%; Calcium 36%; Iron 10% • **Exchanges:** 1 Starch, 1 Milk, 1 High-Fat Meat, 2 Fat • **Carbohydrate Choices:** 1 1/2

Vegetable-Cheese Strata

Savory Sausage and Egg Bake

PREP: 15 MIN; BAKE: 35 MIN

12 servings

1 pound bulk pork sausage

1 1/2 cups sliced mushrooms
(4 ounces)

8 medium green onions, sliced
(1/2 cup)

2 medium tomatoes, chopped
(1 1/2 cups)

2 cups shredded mozzarella
cheese (8 ounces)

1 1/4 cups Original Bisquick mix

1 cup milk

1 teaspoon salt

1/2 teaspoon pepper

12 eggs

1. Heat oven to 350°. Spray bottom and sides of rectangular baking dish, 13 × 9 × 2 inches, with cooking spray. Cook sausage in 10-inch skillet over medium heat, stirring occasionally, until no longer pink; drain. Layer sausage, mushrooms, onions, tomatoes and cheese in dish.

2. Stir remaining ingredients until blended. Pour over cheese.

3. Bake uncovered 30 to 35 minutes or until golden brown and set.

High Altitude (3500 to 6500 feet): Bake about 35 minutes.

Betty's **TIP:** For additional flavor, stir in 1 1/2 teaspoons chopped fresh oregano or 1/2 teaspoon dried oregano leaves with the salt and pepper. This recipe will go together more quickly if you brown the sausage ahead of time; drain, cover and refrigerate.

1 Serving: Calories 255 (Calories from Fat 145); Fat 16g (Saturated 6g); Cholesterol 240mg; Sodium 880mg; Carbohydrate 12g (Dietary Fiber 1g); Protein 17g • **% Daily Value:** Vitamin A 12%; Vitamin C 4%; Calcium 22%; Iron 8% • **Exchanges:** 1 Starch, 2 Medium-Fat Meat, 1/2 Fat • **Carbohydrate** Choices: 1

Country Apple and Sausage Oven Pancake

PREP: 15 MIN; BAKE: 35 MIN

12 servings

1 medium cooking apple,
 thinly sliced

1/2 cup packed brown sugar

1/3 cup butter or margarine

1/2 cup maple-flavored syrup

1 pound bulk pork sausage

1 cup Original Bisquick mix

1/4 cup packed brown sugar

1/2 cup milk

1 egg

1. Heat oven to 350°. Spread apple slices evenly over bottom of ungreased rectangular pan, 13 × 9 × 2 inches. Heat 1/2 cup brown sugar, the butter and syrup in 1-quart saucepan over low heat, stirring occasionally, until melted. Pour syrup mixture over apples.

2. Cook sausage in 10-inch skillet over medium heat, stirring occasionally, until no longer pink; drain. Sprinkle sausage evenly over apple-syrup mixture. Stir remaining ingredients until blended. Carefully pour over sausage.

3. Bake uncovered 30 to 35 minutes or until top springs back when touched in center. Cut into 3-inch squares; turn each square upside down onto plate. Serve immediately with additional syrup if desired.

High Altitude (3500 to 6500 feet): No changes.

Betty's **TIP:** Here's the easy all-in-one way to make pancakes for twelve with all the fixin's—sausage, syrup and even fruit topping. The mild spiciness of the sausage complements the tart apples in this sweet and savory upside-down "pancake."

1 Serving: Calories 265 (Calories from Fat 115); Fat 13g (Saturated 6g); Cholesterol 45mg; Sodium 440mg; Carbohydrate 32g (Dietary Fiber 0g); Protein 5g • **% Daily Value:** Vitamin A 4%; Vitamin C 0%; Calcium 4%; Iron 4% • **Exchanges:** 2 Starch, 2 1/2 Fat • **Carbohydrate Choices:** 2

Do-Ahead Breakfast Bake

PREP: 12 MIN; CHILL: 4 HR; BAKE: 35 MIN; STAND: 10 MIN

12 servings

1 cup diced fully cooked ham
(6 ounces)

2 packages (5.2 ounces each)
hash brown potatoes

1 medium green bell pepper,
chopped (1 cup)

1 tablespoon instant chopped
onion

2 cups shredded Cheddar cheese
(8 ounces)

3 cups milk

1 cup Original or Reduced Fat
Bisquick mix

1/2 teaspoon salt

4 eggs

1. Spray bottom and sides of rectangular baking dish, 13 × 9 × 2 inches, with cooking spray. Mix ham, potatoes, bell pepper, onion and 1 cup of the cheese. Spread in baking dish.

2. Stir milk, Bisquick mix, salt and eggs until blended. Pour over potato mixture. Sprinkle with remaining 1 cup cheese. Cover and refrigerate at least 4 hours but no longer than 24 hours.

3. Heat oven to 375°. Uncover and bake 30 to 35 minutes or until light golden brown around edges and cheese is melted. Let stand 10 minutes before cutting.

High Altitude (3500 to 6500 feet): No changes.

Betty's **TIP:** This is a perfect make-ahead dish for a crowd at breakfast, brunch or dinner. Sprinkle on 1/4 to 1/2 cup bacon-flavor bits or chips with the remaining cheese if desired. Serve with Cinnamon Bubble Loaf (page 18) or Raspberry-Banana Oat Bread (page 20) and a platter of fresh fruit.

1 Serving: Calories 350 (Calories from Fat 110); Fat 12g (Saturated 6g); Cholesterol 100mg; Sodium 610mg; Carbohydrate 45g (Dietary Fiber 3g); Protein 15g • % **Daily Value:** Vitamin A 8%; Vitamin C 8%; Calcium 20%; Iron 6% • **Exchanges:** 3 Starch, 1 Medium-Fat Meat, 2 Fat • **Carbohydrate Choices:** 3

Do-Ahead Breakfast Bake

Bumbleberry Pancakes

PREP: 15 MIN; COOK: 2 TO 3 MIN PER BATCH

About 20 pancakes

2 cups Original Bisquick mix

3/4 cup sour cream

1 cup milk

2 tablespoons sugar

1 egg

1/2 cup fresh or frozen (thawed and drained) raspberries

1/2 cup fresh or frozen (thawed and drained) blueberries

Fruit-flavored syrup or maple syrup, if desired

1. Heat griddle or skillet over medium-high heat (375°); grease with butter if necessary (or spray with cooking spray before heating).

2. Stir all ingredients except berries and syrup in large bowl until blended. Stir in berries. Pour batter by slightly less than 1/4 cupfuls onto hot griddle.

3. Cook until edges are dry. Turn; cook until golden. Serve with syrup.

High Altitude (3500 to 6500 feet): No changes.

Betty's **TIP:** Stack 'em up! The sour cream adds a tangy dairy note to these "berry" yummy pancakes. If you don't have sour cream, use buttermilk or plain yogurt instead.

1 Pancake: Calories 85 (Calories from Fat 35); Fat 4g (Saturated 2g); Cholesterol 15mg; Sodium 180mg; Carbohydrate 10g (Dietary Fiber 0g); Protein 2g • **% Daily Value:** Vitamin A 2%; Vitamin C 0%; Calcium 4%; Iron 2% • **Exchanges:** 1/2 Starch, 1 Fat • **Carbohydrate Choices:** 1/2

Bumbleberry Pancakes

Big Batch Pancakes

PREP: 7 MIN; COOK: 2 MIN 15 SEC PER BATCH

About 90 pancakes

1 package (60 ounces) Original Bisquick mix

12 eggs

7 1/4 cups milk

1. Heat griddle to 375°. (Cooking surface is the proper temperature if pancakes are golden after cooking 1 minute 15 seconds on first side, 1 minute on the second.)

2. Stir all ingredients with wire whisk or hand beater in very large bowl until well blended. Pour batter by scant 1/4 cupfuls or spoon batter by #24 scoop onto hot griddle.

3. Cook until edges are dry. Turn; cook until golden brown.

High Altitude (3500 to 6500 feet): No changes.

Betty's **TIP:** Little ones may prefer theirs mini-sized. Turn part of the batch into silver-dollar size bites by using 1 tablespoon batter for each pancake. To make Big Batch Strawberries and Cream Pancakes, mix 5 cups of strawberries, sliced, and 1 3/4 cups sugar; set aside while making pancakes. Top pancakes with the strawberries and whipped cream.

1 Pancake: Calories 100 (Calories from Fat 35); Fat 4g (Saturated 1g); Cholesterol 30mg; Sodium 300mg; Carbohydrate 13g (Dietary Fiber 0g); Protein 3g • **% Daily Value:** Vitamin A 2%; Vitamin C 0%; Calcium 6%; Iron 4% • **Exchanges:** 1 Starch, 1/2 Fat • **Carbohydrate Choices:** 1

kids LOVE

Big Batch Cheese-Garlic Biscuits
PREP: 10 MIN; BAKE: 10 MIN PER SHEET

Photo on page 150

40 to 48 biscuits

8 cups Original Bisquick mix

2 2/3 cups milk

2 cups shredded Cheddar cheese (8 ounces)

1 cup butter or margarine, melted

1 teaspoon garlic powder

1. Heat oven to 450°. Stir Bisquick mix, milk and cheese until soft dough forms; beat 30 seconds.

2. Drop dough by 40 to 48 spoonfuls about 2 inches apart onto ungreased cookie sheets.

3. Bake 8 to 10 minutes or until golden brown. Mix butter and garlic powder; brush on warm biscuits before removing from cookie sheet. Serve warm.

High Altitude (3500 to 6500 feet): Heat oven to 475°. Bake 9 to 11 minutes.

Betty's **TIP:** You'll probably need to bake one cookie sheet at a time, for best baking results. Prepare the next sheet while the first one bakes. In between batches, keep dough refrigerated so biscuits will be tender and puffy. For Plain Drop Biscuits, omit the cheese, butter and garlic powder.

1 Biscuit: Calories 165 (Calories from Fat 90); Fat 10g (Saturated 5g); Cholesterol 5mg; Sodium 420mg; Carbohydrate 15g (Dietary Fiber 0g); Protein 4g • **% Daily Value:** Vitamin A 4%; Vitamin C 0%; Calcium 8%; Iron 4% • **Exchanges:** 1 Starch, 2 Fat • **Carbohydrate Choices:** 1

Glazed Raisin-Cinnamon Biscuits

PREP: 15 MIN; BAKE: 10 MIN PER BATCH

12 to 15 biscuits

2 1/2 cups Original Bisquick mix

1/2 cup raisins

2/3 cup milk

2 tablespoons granulated sugar

1 teaspoon ground cinnamon

Vanilla Glaze (below)

Vanilla Glaze

2/3 cup powdered sugar

1 tablespoon warm water

1/4 teaspoon vanilla

1. Heat oven to 450°. Stir all ingredients except Vanilla Glaze just until soft dough forms.

2. Place dough on surface generously dusted with Bisquick mix; gently roll in Bisquick mix to coat. Shape into a ball; knead 10 times. Roll 1/2 inch thick. Cut with 2 1/2-inch cutter dipped in Bisquick mix. Place 2 inches inches apart on ungreased cookie sheet.

3. Bake 8 to 10 minutes or until golden brown. While biscuits are baking, make Vanilla Glaze. Spread glaze over warm biscuits.

Vanilla Glaze

Beat all ingredients with spoon until smooth.

High Altitude (3500 to 6500 feet): For rolled biscuits, bake 9 to 11 minutes. For drop biscuits in Betty's Tip, no changes.

Betty's **TIP:** Guess what? You've got a great biscuit cutter on hand if you've got a 2 1/2-inch diameter water glass in your kitchen cabinet. Or save time kneading and rolling and just spoon out drop biscuits onto your ungreased cookie sheet; you may need to increase the baking time to 10 to 12 minutes or until biscuits are golden brown.

1 Biscuit: Calories 165 (Calories from Fat 35); Fat 4g (Saturated 1g); Cholesterol 0mg; Sodium 360mg; Carbohydrate 30g (Dietary Fiber 1g); Protein 2g • **% Daily Value:** Vitamin A 0%; Vitamin C 0%; Calcium 6%; Iron 4% • **Exchanges:** 1 Starch, 1 Other Carbohydrate, 1 Fat • **Carbohydrate Choices:** 2

Glazed Raisin-Cinnamon Biscuits

Mini Rosemary Garlic Focaccias

PREP: 15 MIN; BAKE: 10 MIN

24 mini-focaccias

2 1/4 cups Original Bisquick mix

2/3 cup milk

2 teaspoons olive or vegetable oil

1/2 teaspoon dried rosemary leaves, crumbled

1/2 teaspoon garlic powder

1. Heat oven to 450°. Stir Bisquick mix and milk until soft dough forms; beat 30 seconds. If dough is too sticky, gradually mix in enough Bisquick mix (up to 1/4 cup) to make dough easy to handle.

2. Place dough on surface generously dusted with Bisquick mix; gently roll in Bisquick mix to coat. Shape into a ball; knead 10 times. Roll 1/4 inch thick. Cut with 2-inch cutter dipped in Bisquick mix. Place about 2 inches apart on ungreased cookie sheet. Brush with oil. Sprinkle with rosemary and garlic powder.

3. Bake 8 to 10 minutes or until golden brown. Serve warm.

High Altitude (3500 to 6500 feet): Heat oven to 475°.

Betty's **TIP:** Good quality, shiny aluminum cookie sheets produce the best biscuits or mini-focaccias. If the cookie sheet is brown, black or darkened from a buildup of fat, the bottoms of the biscuits will be darker in color. Placing the cookie sheet on the center oven rack will help your biscuits brown evenly.

1 Biscuit: Calories 55 (Calories from Fat 20); Fat 2g (Saturated 1g); Cholesterol 0mg; Sodium 160mg; Carbohydrate 7g (Dietary Fiber 0g); Protein 1g • **% Daily Value:** Vitamin A 0%; Vitamin C 0%; Calcium 2%; Iron 2% • **Exchanges:** 1/2 Starch, 1/2 Fat • **Carbohydrate Choices:** 1/2

Mini Rosemary Garlic Focaccias

Chapter 6

Hassle-free
HOLIDAYS

Peaches 'n Cream Coffee Cake (page 191) and Hot Cross Biscuits (page 194)

Frosty Snowmen
PREP: 15 MIN; BAKE: 11 MIN

8 servings

2 tablespoons sugar

1 package (3 ounces) cream cheese, softened

1/4 cup firm butter or margarine

2 cups Original Bisquick mix

2 tablespoons sugar

1/2 cup milk

Currants or miniature chocolate chips

Vanilla Glaze (below)

Vanilla Glaze

3/4 cup powdered sugar

1 tablespoon warm water

1/4 teaspoon vanilla

1. Heat oven to 400°. Lightly grease cookie sheet with shortening or spray with cooking spray. Mix 2 tablespoons sugar and the cream cheese; set aside. Cut butter into Bisquick mix and 2 tablespoons sugar in medium bowl, using pastry blender or crisscrossing 2 knives, until mixture looks like coarse crumbs. Stir in milk until dough forms. Place dough on surface sprinkled with Bisquick mix; roll in Bisquick mix to coat. Shape into a ball; knead 10 times. Divide dough into thirds.

2. Divide 2 parts of dough into 4 balls each. Place about 3 inches apart on large cookie sheet for snowmen bodies; flatten slightly. Divide remaining part of dough into 8 balls. Place each ball next to larger round of dough to form snowmen heads; flatten slightly. Make a shallow well in center of each large round of dough with back of spoon; fill with cream cheese mixture. Place currants on snowmen for eyes, nose and buttons.

3. Bake 9 to 11 minutes or until very light golden brown. Drizzle Vanilla Glaze over warm snowmen.

Vanilla Glaze

Mix all ingredients until smooth and thin enough to drizzle. Add 1 to 2 teaspoons more water if necessary.

High Altitude (3500 to 6500 feet): No changes.

Betty's **TIP:** These tasty little snowmen pastries are a fun way to start the day or enjoy for a snack anytime. Kids can help out by rolling the balls of dough and decorating by placing the eyes and buttons on the snowmen. If your family loves spice, try adding 1/2 teaspoon ground cinnamon to the Vanilla Glaze to make it a vanilla-spice glaze.

1 Serving: Calories 305 (Calories from Fat 125); Fat 14g (Saturated 7g); Cholesterol 30mg; Sodium 500mg; Carbohydrate 41g (Dietary Fiber 1g); Protein 4g • **% Daily Value:** Vitamin A 8%; Vitamin C 0%; Calcium 8%; Iron 6% • **Exchanges:** 1 Starch, 2 Other Carbohydrate, 2 1/2 Fat • **Carbohydrate Choices:** 3

Frosty Snowmen

Dilly Blue Beefwiches

PREP: 15 MIN; BAKE: 8 MIN; COOL: 5 MIN

14 servings

2 1/4 cups Original Bisquick mix

2/3 cup milk

1 teaspoon dried dill weed

1/4 cup blue cheese dressing

7 slices thinly sliced deli roast
   beef (6 ounces), cut in half

Leaf lettuce

1. Heat oven to 450°. Stir Bisquick mix, milk and dill weed until soft dough forms.

2. Place dough on surface sprinkled with Bisquick mix; roll in Bisquick mix to coat. Shape into a ball; knead 10 times. Roll dough 1/2 inch thick. Cut with 2-inch round cutter dipped in Bisquick mix. Place 2 inches apart on ungreased cookie sheet.

3. Bake 6 to 8 minutes or until golden brown. Cool at least 5 minutes. Split biscuits in half. Spread slightly less than 1 teaspoon blue cheese dressing on bottom half of each biscuit. Top with folded slice of roast beef and lettuce leaf. Add biscuit top.

High Altitude (3500 to 6500 feet): No changes.

Betty's **TIP:** Red, white and blue colors and flavors make these bite-size sandwiches just right to serve at any summer weekend cookout. If blue cheese dressing isn't to your taste (or the kids'), try using ranch dressing instead.

1 Sandwich: Calories 120 (Calories from Fat 45); Fat 5g (Saturated 1g); Cholesterol 10mg; Sodium 330mg; Carbohydrate 13g (Dietary Fiber 0g); Protein 6g • **% Daily Value:** Vitamin A 2%; Vitamin C 2%; Calcium 6%; Iron 6% • **Exchanges:** 1 Starch, 1/2 Medium-Fat Meat • **Carbohydrate Choices:** 1

Gingerbread Wedges

PREP: 15 MIN; BAKE: 15 MIN

10 wedges

2 1/2 cups Original Bisquick mix

1/4 cup packed brown sugar

1/3 cup full-flavor molasses

1/4 cup whipping (heavy) cream

1/2 teaspoon ground cinnamon

1/2 teaspoon ground ginger

1 egg

Lemon Glaze (below)

Lemon Glaze

1/2 cup powdered sugar

1 tablespoons butter or
    margarine, melted

1 teaspoon grated lemon peel

1 to 2 teaspoons lemon juice

1. Heat oven to 425°. Spray cookie sheet with cooking spray.

2. Stir all ingredients except Lemon Glaze until soft dough forms. Place on surface dusted with Bisquick mix; roll in Bisquick mix to coat. Shape into a ball; knead 10 times. Pat dough into 8-inch circle on cookie sheet. Cut into 10 wedges, but do not separate.

3. Bake 13 to 15 minutes or until set and starting to brown. Make Lemon Glaze; drizzle over wedges. Carefully separate wedges. Serve warm.

Lemon Glaze

Stir together powdered sugar, butter and lemon peel in small bowl. Stir in lemon juice until smooth enough to drizzle.

High Altitude (3500 to 6500 feet): No changes.

Betty's **TIP:** This easy quickbread goes together in no time—it's soon to become a new family dessert favorite! For an extra flavor boost, sprinkle with chopped crystallized ginger or grated lemon peel after glazing.

1 Wedge: Calories 230 (Calories from Fat 72); Fat 8g (Saturated 3g); Cholesterol 30mg; Sodium 450mg; Carbohydrate 37g (Dietary Fiber 0g); Protein 3g • **% Daily Value:** Vitamin A 2%; Vitamin C 0%; Calcium 8%; Iron 8% • **Exchanges:** 1 Starch, 1 1/2 Other Carbohydrates, 1 1/2 Fat • **Carbohydrate Choices:** 2 1/2

Glazed Sweetheart Rolls

PREP: 15 MIN; BAKE: 15 MIN

24 rolls

4 1/2 cups Original Bisquick mix

1 1/3 cups milk

1/4 teaspoon almond extract

2 tablespoons butter or
  margarine, softened

1 package (4-serving size) raspberry-
  or strawberry-flavored gelatin
  (not sugar-free)

Powdered Sugar Icing (below),
  if desired

Powdered Sugar Icing

2 cups powdered sugar

2 to 3 tablespoons milk or water

1 teaspoon vanilla

1. Heat oven to 425°. Line cookie sheet with cooking parchment paper or grease with shortening. Stir Bisquick mix, milk and almond extract until soft dough forms. Place dough on surface generously dusted with Bisquick mix; gently roll in Bisquick mix to coat. Shape into a ball; knead 10 times.

2. Divide dough in half. Roll or pat each half into a 12 × 7-inch rectangle. Spread 1 tablespoon of the butter over each rectangle. Sprinkle half of the gelatin over each rectangle; spread evenly with back of spoon. Roll up each rectangle tightly, beginning at 12-inch side. Pinch edge of dough into roll to seal. Cut each roll into twelve 1-inch slices. Place on cookie sheet. To make heart shape, pinch one side of slice to form sharp point; make deep indentation in opposite side of dough with knife to make top of heart.

3. Bake 12 to 15 minutes or until golden brown. Remove rolls from cookie sheet to wire rack. Spread Powdered Sugar Icing over warm rolls.

Powdered Sugar Icing
Mix all ingredients until smooth and spreadable.

High Altitude (3500 to 6500 feet): Not recommended.

Betty's **TIP:** Perhaps your sweetheart needs a little butterin' up! Serving these rolls for breakfast, brunch or even dessert will help make anyone's day extra special.

1 Roll: Calories 155 (Calories from Fat 35); Fat 4g (Saturated 2g); Cholesterol 5mg; Sodium 340mg; Carbohydrate 28g (Dietary Fiber 0g); Protein 2g • **% Daily Value:** Vitamin A 0%; Vitamin C 0%; Calcium 6%; Iron 4% • **Exchanges:** 1 Starch, 1 Other Carbohydrate, 1/2 Fat • **Carbohydrate Choices:** 2

Glazed Sweetheart Rolls

kids
LOVE

Cupid's Strawberry Shortcakes
PREP: 12 MIN; BAKE: 9 MIN

6 servings

1 pound fresh strawberries
(3 cups), sliced

1/4 cup sugar

2 1/4 cups Original Bisquick mix

1/2 cup milk

2 tablespoons sugar

2 tablespoons butter or
margarine, melted

Pink Whipped Cream (below)

2 tablespoons miniature chocolate
chips

Pink Whipped Cream

1 cup whipping (heavy) cream

3 tablespoons seedless strawberry
preserves

1. Gently stir strawberries and 1/4 cup sugar in medium bowl; refrigerate.

2. Heat oven to 425°. Mix Bisquick mix, milk, 2 tablespoons sugar and the butter until soft dough forms.

3. Place dough on surface sprinkled with Bisquick mix; roll in Bisquick mix to coat. Shape into a ball; knead 10 times. Roll out dough 1/2 inch thick. Cut with 2 1/2-inch heart-shaped cookie cutter dipped in Bisquick mix. Place 2 inches apart on ungreased cookie sheet.

4. Bake 7 to 9 minutes or until golden brown. Split shortcakes. Fill and top with strawberries, Pink Whipped Cream and chocolate chips.

Pink Whipped Cream
Beat whipping cream in chilled small bowl with electric mixer on high speed until soft peaks form. Fold in strawberry preserves.

High Altitude (3500 to 6500 feet): Heat oven to 400°. Use 1/2 cup milk. Bake 12 to 14 minutes.

Betty's **TIP:** You'll be in the pink when you treat your sweetheart to these lovely, special shortcakes. For an extra-special touch, top shortcakes with shaved chocolate curls. Make curls by pulling a vegetable peeler toward you across a milk chocolate candy bar, pressing firmly and using long, thin strokes.

1 Serving: Calories 460 (Calories from Fat 215); Fat 24g (Saturated 12g); Cholesterol 55mg; Sodium 690mg; Carbohydrate 56g (Dietary Fiber 3g); Protein 5g • **% Daily Value:** Vitamin A 12%; Vitamin C 34%; Calcium 12%; Iron 10% • **Exchanges:** 2 Starch, 1 Fruit, 1 Other Carbohydrate, 4 Fat • **Carbohydrate Choices:** 4

Cupid's Strawberry Shortcakes

Cherry-Chocolate Pudding Cake

PREP: 10 MIN; BAKE: 45 MIN

18 servings

1 cup packed brown sugar

1/3 cup baking cocoa

2 cups hot water

2 cups Original Bisquick mix

1 cup granulated sugar

1/4 cup baking cocoa

1/4 cup vegetable oil

1 teaspoon almond extract

2 eggs

1 can (21 ounces) cherry pie filling

Ice cream or whipped cream,
   if desired

1. Heat oven to 350°. Mix brown sugar, 1/3 cup cocoa and the hot water in ungreased rectangular pan, 13 × 9 × 2 inches, until sugar is dissolved.

2. Stir Bisquick mix, granulated sugar, 1/4 cup cocoa, the oil, almond extract and eggs in large bowl until blended. Stir in pie filling. Spoon batter over cocoa mixture in pan.

3. Bake 35 to 45 minutes or until top springs back when touched lightly. Serve warm with ice cream.

High Altitude (3500 to 6500 feet): Bake 40 to 50 minutes.

Betty's **TIP:** Add cherries to the ever-popular chocolate cake that makes its own pudding and it becomes even more appealing. To make it totally irresistible, add a scoop of vanilla ice cream or a spoonful of whipped cream.

1 Serving: Calories 180 (Calories from Fat 55); Fat 6g (Saturated 1g); Cholesterol 25mg; Sodium 200mg; Carbohydrate 30g (Dietary Fiber 2g); Protein 2g • **% Daily Value:** Vitamin A 0%; Vitamin C 0%; Calcium 4%; Iron 6% • **Exchanges:** 1 Starch, 1 Other Carbohydrate, 1 Fat • **Carbohydrate Choices:** 2

Cherry-Chocolate Pudding Cake

Irish Soda Bread

PREP: 14 MIN; BAKE: 25 MIN

12 servings

2 cups Original Bisquick mix

1 tablespoon sugar

1 teaspoon caraway seed

1/2 cup raisins

2/3 cup milk

1 tablespoon butter or margarine, melted, if desired

1. Heat oven to 375°. Spray cookie sheet with cooking spray.

2. Mix Bisquick mix, sugar, caraway seed and raisins in medium bowl. Stir in milk just until dry ingredients are moistened. Place dough on surface sprinkled with Bisquick mix; roll in Bisquick mix to coat. Shape into a ball; knead 10 times. Pat dough into 6-inch round on cookie sheet. Brush with butter.

3. Bake 20 to 25 minutes or until golden brown and bottom sounds hollow when tapped. Remove from pan to wire rack. Serve warm.

High Altitude (3500 to 6500 feet): Bake 23 to 28 minutes.

Betty's **TIP:** Here's the traditional soda bread, made extra easy with Bisquick mix. If you love fruit, leave out caraway and stir in a 4-ounce package of mixed dried fruits with the raisins instead.

1 Slice: Calories 120 (Calories from Fat 35); Fat 4g (Saturated 1g); Cholesterol 5mg; Sodium 300mg; Carbohydrate 19g (Dietary Fiber 1g); Protein 2g • **% Daily Value:** Vitamin A 0%; Vitamin C 0%; Calcium 6%; Iron 4% • **Exchanges:** 1 Starch, 1 Fat • **Carbohydrate Choices:** 1

kids
LOVE

ULTIMATE Peaches 'n Cream Coffee Cake

PREP: 15 MIN; BAKE: 16 MIN

Photo on page 178

6 servings

Peach Filling (below)

1 package (3 ounces) cream cheese

1 tablespoon firm butter or margarine

1 cup Original Bisquick mix

2 tablespoons sugar

1/4 cup milk

1 egg yolk

1 egg white, slightly beaten

2 tablespoons sliced almonds

2 teaspoons sugar

Peach Filling

4 ounces cream cheese (from 8-ounce package), softened

1/2 cup peach preserves

1. Heat oven to 400°. Make Peach Filling. Cut cream cheese and butter into Bisquick mix and 2 tablespoons sugar in medium bowl, using pastry blender or crisscrossing 2 knives, until mixture looks like fine crumbs. Stir in milk and egg yolk until dough forms. Place dough on surface generously dusted with Bisquick mix; gently roll in Bisquick mix to coat. Shape into a ball; knead 10 times.

2. Roll dough into 10-inch circle. Fold circle in half. Place on large ungreased cookie sheet; unfold. Spread filling on dough to within 2 inches of edge. Fold edge of dough over filling. Brush egg white on folded edge; sprinkle with almonds and 2 teaspoons sugar.

3. Bake 14 to 16 minutes or until crust edges are golden brown. Serve warm or cold. Store covered in refrigerator.

Peach Filling
Beat ingredients in small bowl with spoon until smooth and creamy.

High Altitude (3500 to 6500 feet): Use 1 1/2 cups Bisquick mix.

Betty's **TIP:** This Mother's Day, treat your mom and others in your life to this indulgent, easy coffee cake. It's lovely for brunch, but you could also serve it with ice cream for a pretty, fruity dessert.

1 Serving: Calories 340 (Calories from Fat 160); Fat 18g (Saturated 10g); Cholesterol 75mg; Sodium 20mg; Carbohydrate 38g (Dietary Fiber 1g); Protein 6g • **% Daily Value:** Vitamin A 12%; Vitamin C 2%; Calcium 8%; Iron 6% • **Exchanges:** 2 Starch, 1/2 Other Carbohydrate, 3 1/2 Fat • **Carbohydrate Choices:** 2 1/2

Hoppin' Honey Bunny Biscuits

PREP: 15 MIN; BAKE: 10 MIN

About 16 biscuits

3 cups Original Bisquick mix

1/4 teaspoon ground cinnamon

3/4 cup milk

1 package (3 ounces) cream cheese, softened

2 tablespoons honey

2 tablespoons chopped walnuts, if desired

Prepared cinnamon-sugar, if desired

1. Heat oven to 450°. Stir Bisquick mix, cinnamon and milk until soft dough forms; beat vigorously with spoon 30 seconds. Place dough on surface generously dusted with Bisquick mix; gently roll in Bisquick mix to coat. Shape into a ball; knead 10 times.

2. Roll or pat dough into 10 × 8-inch rectangle, 1/2 inch thick. Cut dough lengthwise into 1/2-inch strips. Fold each strip in half into U shape; twist curved end to form lower part of bunny, then twist middle to form upper part of bunny. Leave ends of each strip straight to form bunny ears. Place on ungreased cookie sheet.

3. Make slight indentation in lower circle of dough to hold cream cheese. Mix cream cheese, honey and walnuts. Spoon about 1 teaspoon cream cheese mixture into each indentation for bunny tail. Sprinkle cinnamon-sugar over bunnies. Bake 8 to 10 minutes or until golden brown. Serve warm. Store covered in refrigerator.

High Altitude (3500 to 6500 feet): No changes.

Betty's **TIP:** These are the perfect, easy-to-shape breads to make for Easter or another spring event! Make it a family moment by having the kids help you shape the biscuits; they'll have a good time getting the "honey bunny" shapes just right.

1 Biscuit: Calories 120 (Calories from Fat 45); Fat 5g (Saturated 2g); Cholesterol 5mg; Sodium 340mg; Carbohydrate 17g (Dietary Fiber 0g); Protein 2g • **% Daily Value:** Vitamin A 2%; Vitamin C 0%; Calcium 6%; Iron 4% • **Exchanges:** 1 Starch, 1 Fat • **Carbohydrate Choices:** 1

Hoppin' Honey Bunny Biscuits

Hot Cross Biscuits

PREP: 15 MIN; BAKE: 22 MIN; COOL: 5 MIN

Photo on page 179

16 biscuits

3 cups Original Bisquick mix

3 tablespoons sugar

1/2 teaspoon ground cinnamon

1/4 teaspoon ground nutmeg

1/4 cup dried currants

3/4 cup milk

2 tablespoons butter or margarine, softened

1 tablespoon butter or margarine, melted

Glaze (below)

Glaze

1/2 cup powdered sugar

1 to 2 teaspoons milk

1. Heat oven to 400°. Grease bottom and sides of square pan, 8 × 8 × 2 or 9 × 9 × 2 inches, with shortening or spray with cooking spray. Mix Bisquick mix, sugar, cinnamon, nutmeg and currants in medium bowl. Stir in milk and 2 tablespoons softened butter until dough forms.

2. Place dough on surface dusted with Bisquick mix; gently roll in Bisquick mix to coat. Shape into a ball; knead 10 times. Divide dough into 16 balls; place in pan. Brush with melted butter.

3. Bake 20 to 22 minutes or until golden brown. Cool 5 minutes; remove from pan. Pipe Glaze onto each biscuit in cross pattern. Serve warm.

Glaze

Mix ingredients until smooth and thin enough to drizzle.

High Altitude (3500 to 6500 feet): Bake 22 to 25 minutes.

Betty's **TIP:** These biscuits are perfect for Easter morning or any spring gathering. You can leave out the cinnamon and nutmeg and instead stir in 1/2 teaspoon ground cardamom for a little different flavor.

1 Biscuit: Calories 150 (Calories from Fat 55); Fat 6g (Saturated 2g); Cholesterol 5mg; Sodium 340mg; Carbohydrate 22g (Dietary Fiber 0g); Protein 2g • **% Daily Value:** Vitamin A 2%; Vitamin C 0%; Calcium 6%; Iron 4% • **Exchanges:** 1 Starch, 1/2 Other Carbohydrate, 1 Fat • **Carbohydrate Choices:** 1 1/2

Red, White and Blue Biscuits

PREP: 13 MIN; BAKE: 8 MIN

12 biscuits

2 1/2 cups Original Bisquick mix

1/4 cup chopped, drained, roasted red bell peppers (from 7-ounce jar)

2/3 cup milk

2 tablespoons crumbled blue cheese

1. Heat oven to 450°. Stir all ingredients until soft dough forms.

2. Place dough on surface sprinkled with Bisquick mix; roll in Bisquick mix to coat. Shape into a ball; knead 10 times. Roll out dough 1/2 inch thick. Cut with 3-inch star-shaped cookie cutter dipped in Bisquick mix. Reroll dough to cut remaining biscuits. Place 1 1/2 to 2 inches apart on ungreased cookie sheet.

3. Bake 6 to 8 minutes or until golden brown.

High Altitude (3500 to 6500 feet): No changes.

Betty's **TIP:** Bake and take these savory biscuits to a Fourth of July gathering. With their pretty star shapes, flecked with bits of roasted red pepper, they'll be the talk of the get-together! Remember to wrap them tightly and rewarm when you get there.

1 Biscuit: Calories 110 (Calories from Fat 35); Fat 4g (Saturated 1g); Cholesterol 0mg; Sodium 380mg; Carbohydrate 16g (Dietary Fiber 0g); Protein 2g • **% Daily Value:** Vitamin A 4%; Vitamin C 4%; Calcium 6%; Iron 4% • **Exchanges:** 1 Starch, 1/2 Fat • **Carbohydrate Choices:** 1

kids ♥ LOVE

Spooky Fingers

PREP: 15 MIN; BAKE: 8 MIN PER SHEET; COOL: 17 MIN

20 cookies

3/4 cup powdered sugar

3 tablespoons butter or margarine, softened

1 teaspoon vanilla

1 egg

5 drops yellow food color

3 drops red food color

1 1/2 cups Original Bisquick mix

Chocolate ready-to-spread frosting (from 16-ounce tub), if desired

Red decorating gel (from 0.68-ounce tube), if desired

1. Heat oven to 375°. Mix powdered sugar, butter, vanilla, egg and food colors in large bowl with spoon. Stir in 1 1/4 cups of the Bisquick mix. Shape dough into a ball. Sprinkle remaining 1/4 cup Bisquick mix on countertop or other hard surface. Roll ball of dough in Bisquick mix. Knead dough 10 times.

2. Divide dough into 10 pieces. Roll each piece into 6-inch log, using lightly floured hands. Place about 2 inches apart on ungreased large cookie sheet.

3. Bake 6 to 8 minutes or until set. Cool 2 minutes; remove from cookie sheet to wire rack. Cool completely, about 15 minutes. Cut each strip crosswise in half. Spread frosting over rounded ends of cookies to look like fingernails. Drizzle gel over cut ends of cookies to look like blood.

High Altitude (3500 to 6500 feet): Use 1 tablespoon butter and 1 3/4 cups Bisquick mix (use 1 1/2 cups Bisquick mix in dough). Bake 8 to 10 minutes.

Betty's **TIP:** Halloween is the perfect occasion to have fun with kid baking. Let the little ones get their hands in the dough, then help with the rolling out. Decorating is easy with frosting and gel, so everyone can have a fun—and spooky—time together.

1 Cookie: Calories 100 (Calories from Fat 45); Fat 5g (Saturated 3g); Cholesterol 15mg; Sodium 140mg; Carbohydrate 13g (Dietary Fiber 0g); Protein 1g • **% Daily Value:** Vitamin A 2%; Vitamin C 0%; Calcium 2%; Iron 2% • **Exchanges:** 1 Other Carbohydrate, 1 Fat • **Carbohydrate Choices:** 1

Spooky Fingers

Pumpkin Praline Dessert

PREP: 14 MIN; BAKE: 1 HR; COOL: 20 MIN

12 servings

1 1/2 cups Original Bisquick mix

1/3 cup chopped pecans

1/4 cup butter or margarine

1 can (15 ounces) canned pumpkin
(not pumpkin pie mix)

1/2 cup packed brown sugar

1/3 cup milk

1 teaspoon pumpkin pie spice

3 eggs

Praline Topping (below)

Praline Topping

1/2 cup packed brown sugar

3/4 cup chopped pecans

2 tablespoons Original Bisquick mix

3 tablespoons firm butter or
margarine

1. Heat oven to 350°. Stir together Bisquick mix and pecans in small bowl. Cut in butter, using pastry blender or crisscrossing 2 knives, until crumbly. Press mixture evenly on bottom and up side of ungreased pie plate, 9 × 1 1/4 inches. Bake 9 to 11 minutes or until crust is dry and light golden brown.

2. Stir remaining ingredients except Praline Topping in large bowl with wire whisk or spoon. Pour over crust.

3. Bake 35 minutes. Meanwhile, make Praline Topping. Carefully spoon topping onto pumpkin filling; spread evenly. Bake 10 to 15 minutes longer or until topping is bubbly around edges and pumpkin mixture is set. Cool 20 minutes. Serve warm or cool. Store covered in refrigerator.

Praline Topping
Stir together brown sugar, pecans and Bisquick mix in small bowl. Cut in butter, using pastry blender or crisscrossing 2 knives, until crumbly.

High Altitude (3500 to 6500 feet): Bake crust 11 to 13 minutes. After adding pumpkin mixture, bake 40 minutes.

Betty's **TIP:** This festive dessert offers up the bounty of the fall harvest season in a very easy way. Try using 1 1/2 cups mashed cooked fresh or canned sweet potatoes in place of the pumpkin.

1 Serving: Calories 310 (Calories from Fat 160); Fat 18g (Saturated 6g); Cholesterol 70mg; Sodium 300mg; Carbohydrate 33g (Dietary Fiber 2g); Protein 4g • % **Daily Value:** Vitamin A 100%; Vitamin C 0%; Calcium 8%; Iron 10% • **Exchanges:** 1 1/2 Starch, 1/2 Fruit, 3 1/2 Fat • **Carbohydrate Choices:** 3

Apple-Cranberry Upside-Down Cake

PREP: 15 MIN; BAKE: 35 MIN; STAND: 10 MIN

8 servings

1/4 cup butter or margarine

1/4 cup packed brown sugar

1 medium cooking apple, peeled and sliced

1/2 cup whole berry cranberry sauce

1 1/2 cups Original Bisquick mix

1/2 cup granulated sugar

1/2 cup water or milk

2 tablespoons vegetable oil

1 teaspoon vanilla

1 egg

1. Heat oven to 350°. Melt butter in round pan, 9 × 1 1/2 inches, or square pan, 8 × 8 × 2 inches, in oven. Sprinkle brown sugar over butter. Arrange apple slices in single layer on brown sugar. Spoon cranberry sauce between apple slices.

2. Beat remaining ingredients in large bowl with electric mixer on low speed 30 seconds, scraping bowl constantly. Beat on medium speed 3 minutes, scraping bowl occasionally. Pour batter over apples.

3. Bake 30 to 35 minutes or until toothpick inserted in center of cake comes out clean. Immediately loosen edge of cake by running knife around edge of pan. Place heatproof serving plate upside down onto pan; turn plate and pan over. Leave pan over cake a few minutes. Let cake stand at least 10 minutes before serving.

High Altitude (3500 to 6500 feet): Use 3 tablespoons butter and 1 tablespoon oil. Add 1 tablespoon all-purpose flour with the Bisquick mix. Bake 35 to 45 minutes.

Betty's **TIP:** This warm and homey cake captures the sweet fall flavors of brown sugar, apple and cranberry. You can drizzle some caramel sauce on top and serve with a scoop of ice cream on the side for some extra dessert dazzle.

1 Serving: Calories 295 (Calories from Fat 115); Fat 13g (Saturated 5g); Cholesterol 42mg; Sodium 370mg; Carbohydrate 42g (Dietary Fiber 1g); Protein 2g · **% Daily Value:** Vitamin A 4%; Vitamin C 0%; Calcium 4%; Iron 4% · **Exchanges:** 1 Starch, 2 Other Carbohydrate, 2 Fat · **Carbohydrate Choices:** 3

Gingered Pear Bread

PREP: 12 MIN; BAKE: 1 HR; COOL: 1 HR 10 MIN

1 loaf (16 slices)

1 can (15 ounces) pear halves in syrup, drained and chopped

1/2 cup packed brown sugar

1/4 cup milk

1 tablespoon finely chopped gingerroot

3 tablespoons vegetable oil

2 eggs

3 cups Original Bisquick mix

Ginger Glaze (below)

Finely chopped crystallized ginger, if desired

Ginger Glaze

1/2 cup powdered sugar

2 to 3 teaspoons milk

1 tablespoon finely chopped crystallized ginger

1. Heat oven to 350°. Grease bottom only of loaf pan, 9 × 5 × 3 inches, with shortening or spray bottom with cooking spray.

2. Stir all ingredients except Bisquick mix, Ginger Glaze and crystallized ginger in large bowl until blended. Stir in Bisquick mix until dry ingredients are moistened. Pour into pan.

3. Bake 50 to 60 minutes or until toothpick inserted in center comes out clean. Cool 10 minutes; loosen loaf from sides of pan. Remove from pan to wire rack. Cool completely, about 1 hour. Drizzle with Ginger Glaze; sprinkle with crystallized ginger.

Ginger Glaze

Stir powdered sugar and milk until smooth. Stir in ginger.

High Altitude (3500 to 6500 feet): Use 1/3 cup brown sugar, 1/3 cup milk and 1 tablespoon oil. Add 1 tablespoon all-purpose flour with the Bisquick mix.

Betty's **TIP:** If your family likes sugar and spice, they'll love this beautiful gingery pear bread. It also makes a welcome hostess gift. After cooling completely, wrap in plastic wrap and tie with a colorful ribbon. This bread will keep up to a week when stored tightly wrapped in the refrigerator.

1 Slice: Calories 175 (Calories from Fat 55); Fat 6g (Saturated 1g); Cholesterol 25mg; Sodium 330mg; Carbohydrate 28g (Dietary Fiber 1g); Protein 2g • **% Daily Value:** Vitamin A 0%; Vitamin C 0%; Calcium 4%; Iron 4% • **Exchanges:** 1 Starch, 1 Other Carbohydrate, 1 Fat • **Carbohydrate Choices:** 2

Gingered Pear Bread

Impossibly Easy Eggnog Pie

PREP: 12 MIN; BAKE: 45 MIN; COOL: 1 HR 30 MIN

12 servings

3/4 cup sugar

1 cup whipping (heavy) cream

1 cup milk

2 tablespoons rum or
  1 1/2 teaspoons rum extract

2 teaspoons vanilla

1/2 teaspoon ground nutmeg

4 eggs

1/2 cup Original Bisquick mix

Spiced Whipped Cream (below)

Spiced Whipped Cream

1/2 cup whipping (heavy) cream

1 tablespoon sugar

1/4 teaspoon ground nutmeg

1. Heat oven to 350°. Spray bottom and side of pie plate, 9 × 1 1/4 inches, with cooking spray.

2. Beat all ingredients except Bisquick mix and Spiced Whipped Cream in medium bowl with wire whisk. Stir in Bisquick mix. Pour into pie plate.

3. Bake 42 to 45 minutes or until knife inserted in center comes out clean. Cool completely, about 1 hour 30 minutes. Serve with Spiced Whipped Cream. Store covered in refrigerator.

Spiced Whipped Cream
Beat all ingredients in chilled small bowl with electric mixer on high speed until soft peaks form.

High Altitude (3500 to 6500 feet): Bake 47 to 52 minutes.

Betty's **TIP:** For a colorful and festive dessert, serve with fresh raspberry sauce: Place 1 cup fresh or frozen (thawed and drained) raspberries, 1 tablespoon water and 1 tablespoon sugar in food processor. Cover and process until smooth. Press through sieve to remove seeds if desired.

1 Serving: Calories 200 (Calories from Fat 110); Fat 12g (Saturated 7g); Cholesterol 105mg; Sodium 110mg; Carbohydrate 19g (Dietary Fiber 0g); Protein 4g • **% Daily Value:** Vitamin A 8%; Vitamin C 0%; Calcium 6%; Iron 2% • **Exchanges:** 1 Starch, 2 1/2 Fat • **Carbohydrate Choices:** 1

Impossibly Easy Eggnog Pie

Grasshopper Cheesecake

PREP: 8 MIN; BAKE: 35 MIN; COOL: 45 MIN; CHILL: 3 HR

10 to 12 servings

3/4 cup Original Bisquick mix

3/4 cup sugar

3 to 4 tablespoons crème de menthe

3 eggs

2 packages (8 ounces each) cream cheese, softened

1/4 cup miniature semisweet chocolate chips

Chocolate Ganache (below)

Chocolate Ganache

1/2 cup whipping (heavy) cream

1 cup miniature semisweet chocolate chips

1. Heat oven to 350°. Grease bottom and side of glass pie plate, 9 × 1 1/4 inches, with shortening or spray with cooking spray.

2. Beat all ingredients except chocolate chips and Chocolate Ganache in large bowl with electric mixer on high speed 2 minutes, scraping bowl frequently. Stir in chocolate chips. Pour into pie plate.

3. Bake about 35 minutes or until center is firm and puffed. Cool 45 minutes (cheesecake top will be cracked). Carefully spread Chocolate Ganache over cheesecake. Refrigerate at least 3 hours before serving. Store covered in refrigerator.

Chocolate Ganache

Heat ingredients in 1-quart saucepan over medium heat, stirring constantly, until smooth; remove from heat.

High Altitude (3500 to 6500 feet): No changes.

Betty's **TIP:** This decadent dessert is the perfect do-ahead because it needs to be chilled at least 3 hours before serving. You can substitute crème de menthe-flavored syrup for the 3 tablespoons crème de menthe, but the mint flavor will be a bit milder.

1 Serving: Calories 430 (Calories from Fat 260); Fat 29g (Saturated 17g); Cholesterol 125mg; Sodium 290mg; Carbohydrate 37g (Dietary Fiber 1g); Protein 7g • **% Daily Value:** Vitamin A 16%; Vitamin C 0%; Calcium 6%; Iron 8% • **Exchanges:** 2 Starch, 1/2 Other Carbohydrate, 5 1/2 Fat • **Carbohydrate Choices:** 2 1/2

Grasshopper Cheesecake

Nutty Noel Bars

PREP: 15 MIN; BAKE: 18 MIN; COOL: 1 HR

32 bars

1 1/2 cups Original Bisquick mix

1 cup old-fashioned or quick-cooking oats

3/4 cup packed brown sugar

1/3 cup butter or margarine, softened

1 egg

1 1/4 cups white baking chips

2 tablespoons whipping (heavy) cream

1 1/2 cups mixed nuts or cashews

1. Heat oven to 350°. Lightly grease bottom only of rectangular pan, 13 × 9 × 2 inches, with shortening or spray bottom with cooking spray.

2. Stir Bisquick mix, oats, brown sugar, butter and egg in large bowl until well blended. Press on bottom of pan. Bake 16 to 18 minutes or until golden brown.

3. Place white baking chips and whipping cream in small micro-wavable bowl. Microwave uncovered on Medium-High (70%) 1 minute; stir. Microwave 10 to 15 seconds longer or until mixture can be stirred smooth. Spread over baked layer. Sprinkle with nuts; press gently into topping. Cool completely, about 1 hour. For bars, cut into 8 rows by 4 rows.

High Altitude (3500 to 6500 feet): No changes.

Betty's **TIP:** There's a treasure chest of crunchy goodness in these sweet and salty nutty bars. You can use salted pecan halves or peanuts in place of the mixed nuts. Keep bars tightly covered at room temperature, or freeze up to 3 months.

1 Cookie: Calories 175 (Calories from Fat 90); Fat 10g (Saturated 4g); Cholesterol 15mg; Sodium 40mg; Carbohydrate 18g (Dietary Fiber 1g); Protein 3g • **% Daily Value:** Vitamin A 2%; Vitamin C 0%; Calcium 4%; Iron 4% • **Exchanges:** 1 Starch, 2 Fat • **Carbohydrate Choices:** 1

Nutty Noel Bars

Brandy Crème Brûlée Dessert

PREP: 15 MIN; BAKE: 1 HR 8 MIN; COOL: 1 HR

12 servings

3 tablespoons butter or margarine, softened

1 1/4 cups Original Bisquick mix

1/3 cup sugar

5 egg yolks

1/4 cup sugar

1 1/4 cups whipping (heavy) cream

1 tablespoon plus 1 teaspoon brandy or 1 1/2 teaspoons brandy extract

1/3 cup sugar

1. Heat oven to 350°. Cut butter into Bisquick mix and 1/3 cup sugar in medium bowl, using pastry blender or crisscrossing 2 knives, until well mixed. Press on bottom and 1/2 inch up sides of ungreased square pan, 9 × 9 × 2 inches. Bake 16 to 18 minutes or until golden brown; remove from oven.

2. Reduce oven temperature to 300°. Beat egg yolks and 1/4 cup sugar in small bowl with wire whisk until thick. Gradually stir in whipping cream and brandy until blended. Pour over baked layer. Bake 40 to 50 minutes or until custard is set and toothpick inserted in center comes out clean. Cool completely, about 1 hour.

3. For serving pieces, cut into 4 rows by 3 rows. Place on dessert plates. Heat 1/3 cup sugar in heavy 1-quart saucepan over medium heat until sugar begins to melt. Stir until sugar is completely dissolved and caramel colored. Cool slightly until caramel has thickened slightly. Quickly drizzle hot caramel evenly over each serving. (If caramel begins to harden, return to medium heat and stir until thin enough to drizzle.) Store dessert covered in refrigerator.

High Altitude (3500 to 6500 feet): Use 2 tablespoons butter.

Betty's **TIP:** To make bite-size Crème Brûlée Dessert Bars, cut into 8 rows by 6 rows. It's the perfect size for holiday snacking.

1 Serving: Calories 235 (Calories from Fat 125); Fat 14g (Saturated 8g); Cholesterol 125mg; Sodium 210mg; Carbohydrate 24g (Dietary Fiber 0g); Protein 3g • **% Daily Value:** Vitamin A 10%; Vitamin C 0%; Calcium 4%; Iron 4% • **Exchanges:** 1 Starch, 1/2 Other Carbohydrate, 3 Fat • **Carbohydrate Choices:** 1 1/2

Triple-Chocolate Crinkles

PREP: 12 MIN; BAKE: 10 MIN PER SHEET; COOL: 20 MIN

About 28 cookies

2 cups Original Bisquick mix

1 cup packed brown sugar

1/3 cup baking cocoa

2 tablespoons butter or margarine, melted

2 eggs

3/4 cup semisweet chocolate chips

1/2 cup white baking chips

1/2 teaspoon shortening

1. Heat oven to 350°. Mix Bisquick mix, brown sugar and cocoa in large bowl. Stir in butter and eggs until soft dough forms. Stir in chocolate chips.

2. Shape dough into 1-inch balls. Place about 2 inches apart on ungreased cookie sheet. Bake 8 to 10 minutes or until set. Cool 1 minute; remove from cookie sheet to wire rack. Cool completely, about 20 minutes.

3. Melt white baking chips and shortening in small microwavable bowl uncovered on Medium-High (70%) 1 minute; stir. Continue to microwave 10 seconds at a time, stirring after each time, until chips can be stirred smooth. Spoon into resealable plastic food-storage bag. Cut very small tip from corner of bag. Drizzle over cookies.

High Altitude (3500 to 6500 feet): No changes.

Betty's **TIP:** Remember chocolate crinkles from your childhood? Here they are, made extra easy and triple good with your homemade ingredients. They'll be the hit of the next school bake sale!

1 Cookie: Calories 130 (Calories from Fat 45); Fat 5g (Saturated 3g); Cholesterol 20mg; Sodium 40mg; Carbohydrate 19g (Dietary Fiber 1g); Protein 2g • **% Daily Value:** Vitamin A 0%; Vitamin C 0%; Calcium 4%; Iron 4% • **Exchanges:** 1 Starch, 1 Fat • **Carbohydrate Choices:** 1

Sugarplum Cookie Pizza

PREP: 15 MIN; BAKE: 11 MIN; COOL: 30 MIN; STAND: 20 MIN

16 servings

1/2 cup sugar

1/4 cup shortening

2 teaspoons grated orange peel

1 egg

1 1/3 cups Original Bisquick mix

1/2 cup vanilla ready-to-spread
   frosting (from 16-ounce tub)

1 1/2 cups small gumdrops

1/2 cup white baking chips

1 teaspoon shortening

1. Heat oven to 350°. Grease 12-inch pizza pan with shortening or spray with cooking spray. Mix sugar, 1/4 cup shortening, the orange peel and egg in large bowl with spoon. Stir in Bisquick mix until dough forms. Spread or pat dough on bottom and up side of pan.

2. Bake 10 to 11 minutes or until crust is light golden and set. Cool in pan 30 minutes.

3. Spread frosting over cookie crust. Top with gumdrops. Melt white baking chips and 1 teaspoon shortening in small microwavable bowl uncovered on Medium-High (70%) 1 minute; stir. Continue to microwave 10 seconds at a time, stirring after each time, until chips can be stirred smooth. Drizzle over cookie. Let stand 15 to 20 minutes or until topping is set. To serve, cut into wedges.

High Altitude (3500 to 6500 feet): No changes.

Betty's **TIP:** Kids of all ages will love making and eating this sweet pizza, with its kaleidoscope of colors. Bake in a disposable pizza pan, and give as a hostess gift. Instead of gumdrops, top with jelly beans or other soft, chewy candies.

1 Serving: Calories 255 (Calories from Fat 80); Fat 9g (Saturated 4g); Cholesterol 15mg; Sodium 160mg; Carbohydrate 41g (Dietary Fiber 0g); Protein 2g • **% Daily Value:** Vitamin A 0%; Vitamin C 0%; Calcium 4%; Iron 2% • **Exchanges:** 1 Starch, 2 Other Carbohydrate, 1 Fat • **Carbohydrate Choices:** 3

Sugarplum Cookie Pizza

Chapter 7

DESSERTS,
Cookies and

Chocolate Waffle Cookies (page 227) and Lemon Bread Pudding (page 218)

Bars

Strawberry-Banana Crepes

PREP: 15 MIN; COOK: 9 MIN

12 servings

Crepes (below)

1 1/2 cups whipping (heavy) cream

1/4 cup sugar

2 to 3 bananas, sliced

1 pint (2 cups) fresh strawberries, sliced, or 1 package (10 ounces) frozen strawberries, partially thawed

1/4 cup chopped walnuts

Crepes

1 cup Original Bisquick mix

3/4 cup milk

2 eggs

1. Make Crepes.

2. Beat whipping cream and sugar in chilled medium bowl with electric mixer on high speed until soft peaks form. Spoon about 3 tablespoons whipped cream down center of each crepe; top with 4 or 5 banana slices. Roll up; place seam sides down on serving plate. Top each crepe with dollop of whipped cream, strawberries and walnuts.

Crepes

Stir all ingredients until blended. Lightly spray 6- or 7-inch non-stick skillet with cooking spray; heat over medium-high heat. For each crepe, pour 2 tablespoons batter into skillet; rotate skillet until batter covers bottom. Cook until golden brown. Gently loosen edge with metal spatula; turn and cook other side until golden brown. Stack crepes as you remove them from skillet, placing waxed paper between them. Keep crepes covered to prevent them from drying out.

High Altitude (3500 to 6500 feet): No changes.

Betty's **TIP:** Use whatever berries you have on hand—raspberries, blueberries, blackberries or a combination. All will be delicious with these thin, lacy crepes. The crepes can be frozen up to 3 months. Stack cool, unfilled crepes with waxed paper between them. Wrap the stack in aluminum foil or place in an airtight plastic freezer bag; label and freeze. Thaw at room temperature about 1 hour or in refrigerator 6 to 8 hours. Warm each crepe about 10 seconds in microwave before filling.

1 Crepe: Calories 220 (Calories from Fat 125); Fat 14g (Saturated 7g); Cholesterol 70mg; Sodium 170mg; Carbohydrate 20g (Dietary Fiber 1g); Protein 4g · **% Daily Value:** Vitamin A 8%; Vitamin C 12%; Calcium 6%; Iron 4% · **Exchanges:** 1 Starch, 1/2 Fruit, 2 1/2 Fat · **Carbohydrate Choices:** 1

Strawberry-Banana Crepes

kids LOVE

Chocolate-Cherry Crisp

PREP: 10 MIN; BAKE: 35 MIN

9 or 10 servings

1 can (21 ounces) cherry pie filling

1/2 cup Original Bisquick mix

1/2 cup packed brown sugar

1/2 cup quick-cooking oats

1/4 cup firm butter or margarine

1/2 cup semisweet chocolate chips

1. Heat oven to 350°. Spread pie filling in ungreased square pan, 8 × 8 × 2 inches.

2. Stir together Bisquick mix, brown sugar and oats in medium bowl. Cut in butter, using pastry blender or crisscrossing 2 knives, until crumbly. Stir in chocolate chips. Spoon evenly over pie filling.

3. Bake 30 to 35 minutes or until very bubbly around edges. Serve warm.

High Altitude (3500 to 6500 feet): Use 3/4 cup Bisquick mix. Bake 35 to 40 minutes.

Betty's **TIP:** Strawberry and raspberry pie fillings are great stand-ins for the cherry pie filling. Take this easy crisp to your next potluck. Double the recipe and bake in a 13 × 9-inch pan for a real crowd pleaser.

1 Serving: Calories 255 (Calories from Fat 80); Fat 9g (Saturated 5g); Cholesterol 15mg; Sodium 140mg; Carbohydrate 41g (Dietary Fiber 2g); Protein 2g • **% Daily Value:** Vitamin A 4%; Vitamin C 0%; Calcium 2%; Iron 6% • **Exchanges:** 1 Starch, 1 Fruit, 1 Other Carbohydrate, 1 Fat • **Carbohydrate Choices:** 3

Chocolate-Cherry Crisp

Lemon Bread Pudding

PREP: 14 MIN; BAKE: 50 MIN

Photo on page 213

9 or 10 servings

1/2 cup sugar

1/2 teaspoon vanilla

6 eggs

1/2 cup Original Bisquick mix

2 cups milk

10 cups cubed French bread
(about ten 1-inch slices)

1 can (15 3/4 ounces) lemon pie
filling or any fruit pie filling

1 cup frozen (thawed) whipped
topping

1. Heat oven to 350°. Generously grease bottom and side of 3-quart casserole with shortening or spray with cooking spray. Beat sugar, vanilla and eggs in large bowl with wire whisk until blended. Stir in Bisquick mix and milk. Stir in bread cubes until coated.

2. Spoon half of the bread mixture into casserole. Spoon 1 cup of the pie filling randomly over bread mixture. Top with remaining bread mixture.

3. Bake 45 to 50 minutes or until golden brown and knife inserted in center comes out clean. Mix remaining pie filling and the whipped topping. Serve warm pudding with whipped topping mixture. Store covered in refrigerator.

High Altitude (3500 to 6500 feet): Heat oven to 375°. Bake 50 to 55 minutes.

Betty's **TIP:** You can bake and serve warm pudding and still have the convenience of making it ahead. Just cover and refrigerate unbaked bread pudding up to 24 hours before baking. For a special touch, sprinkle white coarse sugar crystals (decorating sugar) over bread pudding before baking.

1 Serving: Calories 310 (Calories from Fat 70); Fat 8g (Saturated 3g); Cholesterol 145mg; Sodium 390mg; Carbohydrate 50g (Dietary Fiber 2g); Protein 10g • **% Daily Value:** Vitamin A 6%; Vitamin C 0%; Calcium 12%; Iron 10% • **Exchanges:** 3 Starch, 1 1/2 Fat • **Carbohydrate Choices:** 3

Candied Apple Tart

PREP: 15 MIN; BAKE: 20 MIN

10 servings

2 cups Original Bisquick mix

2/3 cup whipping (heavy) cream

2 tablespoons granulated sugar

4 cups thinly sliced cooking apples (about 4 medium)

1/4 cup Original Bisquick mix

1/3 cup packed brown sugar

1 tablespoon firm butter or margarine

3/4 teaspoon ground cinnamon

About 2 tablespoons cinnamon apple jelly

1. Heat oven to 425°. Stir 2 cups Bisquick mix, the whipping cream and granulated sugar until soft dough forms; shape into a ball. Pat dough in ungreased 12-inch pizza pan. Spread apples over dough.

2. Mix 1/4 cup Bisquick mix, the brown sugar, butter and cinnamon with fork until crumbly; sprinkle over apples. Cover edge of dough with 2-inch strip of aluminum foil to prevent excessive browning.

3. Bake 5 minutes; remove foil. Bake 10 to 15 minutes longer or until edge is deep golden brown. Heat jelly until melted; drizzle over tart.

High Altitude (3500 to 6500 feet): Increase second bake time to 15 to 20 minutes.

Betty's **TIP:** This tart will be just as "a-peeling" if you leave the peels on the apples. Apple peel adds color (plus some fiber!) to this pretty pie. If caramel apple tart sounds good to you and your family, leave off the cinnamon apple jelly and drizzle with caramel topping.

1 Serving: Calories 240 (Calories from Fat 90); Fat 10g (Saturated 5g); Cholesterol 20mg; Sodium 400mg; Carbohydrate 36g (Dietary Fiber 2g); Protein 2g • **% Daily Value:** Vitamin A 4%; Vitamin C 2%; Calcium 6%; Iron 6% • **Exchanges:** 1 Starch, 1/2 Fruit, 1 Other Carbohydrate, 2 Fat • **Carbohydrate Choices:** 2 1/2

kids LOVE

Banana-Coconut Cream Dessert

PREP: 15 MIN; BAKE: 15 MIN; COOL: 30 MIN; CHILL: 1 HR

16 servings

2 cups Original Bisquick mix

2 tablespoons sugar

1/4 cup firm butter or margarine

1 package (4-serving size) vanilla instant pudding and pie filling mix

1 3/4 cups milk

2 medium bananas, sliced

2 cups whipped cream

1/2 cup toasted shredded coconut

1. Heat oven to 375°. Mix Bisquick mix and sugar in medium bowl. Cut in butter, using pastry blender or crisscrossing 2 knives, until crumbly. Press in bottom of ungreased square pan, 9 × 9 × 2 inches.

2. Bake about 15 minutes or until light brown. Cool completely, about 30 minutes.

3. Make pudding mix as directed on package for pudding, using 1 3/4 cups milk; spread over crust. Top with banana slices. Spread whipped cream over top. Sprinkle with coconut. Cover and refrigerate at least 1 hour but no longer than 24 hours.

High Altitude (3500 to 6500 feet): No changes.

Betty's **TIP:** The flavors will develop after chilling for at least 1 hour. This is a great do-ahead dessert; make it first thing in the morning and let it chill for a special dinner.

1 Serving: Calories 245 (Calories from Fat 145); Fat 16g (Saturated 9g); Cholesterol 45mg; Sodium 350mg; Carbohydrate 23g (Dietary Fiber 1g); Protein 3g • **% Daily Value:** Vitamin A 10%; Vitamin C 2%; Calcium 8%; Iron 2% • **Exchanges:** 1 Starch, 1/2 Fruit, 3 Fat • **Carbohydrate Choices:** 1 1/2

Banana-Coconut Cream Dessert

Raspberry-Peach Cobbler

PREP: 15 MIN; BAKE: 45 MIN

9 servings

2 1/2 cups sliced fresh peaches

2 cups fresh raspberries

1/2 cup granulated sugar

1 tablespoon cornstarch

1 teaspoon ground nutmeg

2 cups Original Bisquick mix

1/2 cup milk

3 tablespoons butter or
   margarine, melted

2 tablespoons granulated sugar
   or packed brown sugar

1. Heat oven to 375°. Lightly butter bottom and side of deep-dish pie plate, 9 × 1 1/2 inches.

2. Mix peaches, raspberries, 1/2 cup granulated sugar, cornstarch and nutmeg in large bowl. Let stand 10 minutes. Spoon into pie plate.

3. Stir remaining ingredients in same bowl until dough forms. Drop dough by spoonfuls onto fruit mixture. Bake 37 to 45 minutes or until fruit is bubbly and topping is deep golden brown and baked through.

High Altitude (3500 to 6500 feet): No changes.

Betty's **TIP:** You don't have to save this fantastically fruity dessert for summer only. Make it with frozen sliced peaches and raspberries, thawed and drained, in any season.

1 Serving: Calories 245 (Calories from Fat 70); Fat 8g (Saturated 3g); Cholesterol 10mg; Sodium 0mg; Carbohydrate 40g (Dietary Fiber 3g); Protein 3g • **% Daily Value:** Vitamin A 4%; Vitamin C 16%; Calcium 6%; Iron 6% • **Exchanges:** 1 Starch, 1 Fruit, 1/2 Other Carbohydrate, 2 Fat • **Carbohydrate Choices:** 2 1/2

Raspberry-Peach Cobbler

Saucy Apple Gingerbread

PREP: 14 MIN; BAKE: 38 MIN

10 to 12 servings

1/4 cup butter or margarine,
  melted

1/2 cup packed brown sugar

1 can (21 ounces) apple pie filling

2 cups Original Bisquick mix

1/3 cup packed brown sugar

1/4 cup butter or margarine,
  softened

3/4 cup water

1/3 cup molasses

1 teaspoon ground allspice

1 teaspoon ground ginger

1 egg

1. Heat oven to 350°. Mix melted butter, 1/2 cup brown sugar and the pie filling. Spoon into ungreased square pan, 9 × 9 × 2 inches. Place in oven while making batter.

2. Beat remaining ingredients in large bowl with electric mixer on low speed 30 seconds, scraping bowl constantly. Beat on medium speed 2 minutes, scraping bowl occasionally. Pour over warm apple filling.

3. Bake 34 to 38 minutes or until toothpick inserted in center of gingerbread comes out clean and top is cracked. Spoon into bowls; serve warm.

High Altitude (3500 to 6500 feet): Heat oven to 375°. Bake 39 to 43 minutes.

Betty's **TIP:** Use dark brown sugar and full-flavor molasses for a gingerbread with a richer flavor and color. Peach or apricot pie filling makes a tasty substitution for the apple pie filling. Top warm gingerbread with cinnamon ice cream or whipped topping.

1 Serving: Calories 315 (Calories from Fat 115); Fat 13g (Saturated 7g); Cholesterol 45mg; Sodium 420mg; Carbohydrate 47g (Dietary Fiber 1g); Protein 3g • **% Daily Value:** Vitamin A 8%; Vitamin C 0%; Calcium 8%; Iron 8% • **Exchanges:** 1 Starch, 1 Fruit, 1 Other Carbohydrate, 2 1/2 Fat • **Carbohydrate Choices:** 3

Saucy Apple Gingerbread

Mocha Chip Biscotti

PREP: 15 MIN; BAKE: 35 MIN; COOL: 40 MIN

About 3 dozen cookies

1 tablespoon instant espresso coffee or coffee crystals (dry)

1 teaspoon hot water

1/2 cup packed brown sugar

3 tablespoons butter or margarine, softened

1/2 teaspoon vanilla

1 egg

1 3/4 cups Original Bisquick mix

1/2 cup chopped pecans

1/4 cup miniature semisweet chocolate chips

1. Heat oven to 350°. Dissolve instant coffee in the hot water. Beat brown sugar, butter, vanilla, egg and coffee in large bowl with electric mixer on medium speed about 1 minute or until blended. Stir in remaining ingredients. Place dough on surface sprinkled with Bisquick mix; gently roll in Bisquick mix to coat. Divide dough in half. Shape each half into a 10 × 3-inch rectangle on ungreased cookie sheet.

2. Bake 20 to 25 minutes or until cracked and deep brown around edges. Cool on cookie sheet 10 minutes. Cut each rectangle crosswise into 1/2-inch slices. Carefully turn slices cut side down on cookie sheet.

3. Bake 8 to 10 minutes or until crisp and deep brown around edges. Cool on cookie sheet 5 minutes; carefully remove from cookie sheet to wire rack. Cool completely, about 25 minutes.

High Altitude (3500 to 6500 feet): No changes.

Betty's **TIP:** Dip biscotti in melted chocolate for a coffee-shop fancy finish. Melt chocolate by heating 1 cup chocolate chips and 1 teaspoon shortening over low heat, stirring frequently. Plain biscotti keep for up to a week in an airtight container, or they can be frozen up to 2 months before serving.

1 Cookie: Calories 65 (Calories from Fat 25); Fat 3g (Saturated 1g); Cholesterol 10mg; Sodium 90mg; Carbohydrate 8g (Dietary Fiber 0g); Protein 1g • **% Daily Value:** Vitamin A 0%; Vitamin C 0%; Calcium 2%; Iron 2% • **Exchanges:** 1/2 Starch, 1/2 Fat • **Carbohydrate Choices:** 1/2

Chocolate Waffle Cookies
PREP: 10 MIN; BAKE: 3 MIN PER BATCH

Photo on page 212

About 2 dozen 2-inch cookies

1/3 cup semisweet chocolate chips

1/4 cup butter or margarine

1 cup Original Bisquick mix

1/4 cup granulated sugar

1/4 cup milk

1 teaspoon vanilla

1 egg

About 1/2 cup semisweet chocolate chips

Powdered sugar, if desired

1. Heat waffle iron to medium-high (spray with cooking spray before heating if necessary). Heat 1/3 cup chocolate chips and the butter in 1 1/2-quart saucepan over low heat, stirring constantly, until melted. Stir in remaining ingredients except 1/2 cup chocolate chips and the powdered sugar.

2. Drop 1 tablespoon batter onto each section of ungreased waffle iron. Close lid of waffle iron. Bake 2 to 3 minutes or until steaming stops.

3. Remove from waffle iron to wire rack. Immediately sprinkle each cookie with about 1 teaspoon chocolate chips and powdered sugar. Serve warm.

High Altitude (3500 to 6500 feet): Bake 3 to 4 minutes.

Betty's **TIP:** Drizzle cookies with a glaze made by melting 1/2 cup chocolate chips with 2 teaspoons shortening, and sprinkle with chopped nuts. Or sandwich a scoop of ice cream between two waffle cookies and press slightly to make ice-cream sandwiches.

1 Cookie: Calories 85 (Calories from Fat 45); Fat 5g (Saturated 3g); Cholesterol 15mg; Sodium 90mg; Carbohydrate 9g (Dietary Fiber 0g); Protein 1g • % **Daily Value:** Vitamin A 2%; Vitamin C 0%; Calcium 2%; Iron 2% • **Exchanges:** 1/2 Starch, 1 Fat • **Carbohydrate Choices:** 1/2

P B and J Strips

PREP: 15 MIN; BAKE: 11 MIN; COOL: 5 MIN

About 4 dozen cookies

1/2 cup granulated sugar

1/2 cup packed brown sugar

1/2 cup peanut butter

1/4 cup shortening

1 egg

1 3/4 cups Original Bisquick mix

1/3 cup strawberry jam or preserves

1. Heat oven to 375°. Beat sugars, peanut butter, shortening and egg in large bowl with electric mixer on low speed 30 seconds, scraping bowl constantly. Beat on medium speed 1 minute, scraping bowl occasionally. Stir in Bisquick mix until blended.

2. Place dough on surface sprinkled with Bisquick mix; gently roll in Bisquick mix to coat. Divide dough into 4 parts. Shape each part into roll 3/4 inch in diameter and about 13 inches long. Place rolls about 2 inches apart on large ungreased cookie sheet.

3. Make indentation lengthwise in center of each roll with handle of wooden spoon. Spoon jam into resealable plastic food-storage bag; cut very small (1/4-inch) tip from corner of bag. Squeeze preserves evenly into indentations.

4. Bake 9 to 11 minutes until light golden brown and set. Cool on cookie sheet 5 minutes. Cut each roll into 12 slices. Remove from cookie sheet to wire rack.

High Altitude (3500 to 6500 feet): Bake 11 to 14 minutes.

Betty's **TIP:** Kids will love grape jelly instead of the strawberry jam. For a special touch, drizzle cookies with Vanilla Glaze (page 231).

1 Cookie: Calories 65 (Calories from Fat 25); Fat 3g (Saturated 1g); Cholesterol 5mg; Sodium 80mg; Carbohydrate 9g (Dietary Fiber 0g); Protein 1g • **% Daily Value:** Vitamin A 0%; Vitamin C 0%; Calcium 0%; Iron 0% • **Exchanges:** 1/2 Starch, 1/2 Fat • **Carbohydrate Choices:** 1/2

P B and J Strips

Monster Cookies

PREP: 15 MIN; BAKE: 16 MIN PER SHEET; COOL: 3 MIN

About 1 1/2 dozen 3 1/2-inch cookies

1 1/4 cups packed brown sugar

1/2 cup shortening

2 eggs

2 1/2 cups Original Bisquick mix

1 cup old-fashioned or quick-cooking oats

1 cup candy-coated chocolate candies

1/2 cup raisins

1/2 cup chopped nuts, if desired

Granulated sugar, if desired

1. Heat oven to 375°. Beat brown sugar, shortening and eggs in large bowl with electric mixer on medium speed, or mix with spoon. Stir in remaining ingredients, except granulated sugar.

2. Drop dough by 1/4 cupfuls about 2 inches apart onto ungreased cookie sheet. Flatten to about 1/2-inch thickness with bottom of glass that has been greased and dipped into granulated sugar.

3. Bake 12 to 16 minutes or until golden brown. Cool 3 minutes; carefully remove from cookie sheet to wire rack.

High Altitude (3500 to 6500 feet): Bake 11 to 14 minutes.

Betty's **TIP:** Cookie monsters will love biting into these jumbo-sized cookies, chock-full of fun add-ins. Any chopped dried fruit—dried cranberries, apricots or dates—can replace the raisins. They're perfect for gift-giving too; stack cookies in a see-through gift bag, and tie with colorful ribbons.

1 Cookie: Calories 270 (Calories from Fat 100); Fat 11g (Saturated 4g); Cholesterol 25mg; Sodium 260mg; Carbohydrate 40g (Dietary Fiber 1g); Protein 3g • **% Daily Value:** Vitamin A 0%; Vitamin C 0%; Calcium 6%; Iron 6% • **Exchanges:** 1 Starch, 1 1/2 Other Carbohydrates, 2 Fat • **Carbohydrate Choices:** 2 1/2

Glazed Apricot Jam Strips

PREP: 15 MIN; BAKE: 14 MIN

32 cookies

1/4 cup packed brown sugar

2 tablespoons shortening

2 tablespoons butter or
margarine, softened

1/2 teaspoon vanilla

1 egg yolk

1 1/2 cups Original Bisquick mix

1/3 cup apricot preserves

Vanilla Glaze (below)

Vanilla Glaze

1/2 cup powdered sugar

1 to 2 teaspoons milk

1. Heat oven to 350°. Mix brown sugar, shortening, butter, vanilla and egg yolk with spoon in medium bowl. Stir in Bisquick mix until well blended.

2. Divide dough into 4 equal parts. Shape each part into 8 × 1-inch strip crosswise on ungreased cookie sheet. Make slight indentation lengthwise in each strip with handle of wooden spoon. Fill each indentation with about 1 1/2 tablespoons of the preserves.

3. Bake 12 to 14 minutes or until edges are light brown; cool slightly on cookie sheet. Drizzle with Vanilla Glaze. Cut diagonally into 1-inch strips.

Vanilla Glaze
Mix ingredients until smooth and thin enough to drizzle.

High Altitude (3500 to 6500 feet): Heat oven to 375°. Use 2 tablespoons brown sugar. Add 2 tablespoons all-purpose flour with the Bisquick mix.

Betty's **TIP:** When it comes to baking, not all fats are created equal. Shortening, butter and stick margarine are fine; if you use a vegetable oil spread, make sure it has at least 65% fat, and avoid baking with tub margarines and whipped products.

1 Cookie: Calories 60 (Calories from Fat 20); Fat 2g (Saturated 1g); Cholesterol 10mg; Sodium 85mg; Carbohydrate 9g (Dietary Fiber 0g); Protein 1g • **% Daily Value:** Vitamin A 0%; Vitamin C 0%; Calcium 0%; Iron 0% • **Exchanges:** 1/2 Starch, 1/2 Fat • **Carbohydrate Choices:** 1/2

ULTIMATE Sugar Cookie Cut-Ups

PREP: 15 MIN; BAKE: 8 MIN PER SHEET; COOL: 15 MIN

About 1 1/2 dozen cookies

1/3 cup powdered sugar

3 tablespoons shortening

3 tablespoons butter or margarine, softened

1 teaspoon vanilla

1 egg yolk

1 1/2 ounces cream cheese (from 3-ounce package), softened

1 1/2 cups Original Bisquick mix

1 tub (16 ounces) vanilla ready-to-spread frosting, if desired

1. Heat oven to 375°. Grease cookie sheet with shortening or spray with cooking spray. Stir all ingredients except Bisquick mix and frosting in large bowl with spoon until well blended. Stir in Bisquick mix until dough forms.

2. Roll out half of the dough at a time on surface sprinkled with powdered sugar until 1/4 inch thick. Cut into 2-inch square or diamond shapes with pizza cutter. Place about 1 inch apart on cookie sheet.

3. Bake 6 to 8 minutes or until edges are light golden brown. Carefully remove from cookie sheet to wire rack. Cool completely, about 15 minutes. Spread with frosting.

High Altitude (3500 to 6500 feet): No changes.

Betty's **TIP:** Shape these cookies freehand with a pizza wheel or sharp knife, or use 2-inch cookie cutters in your favorite shapes. Baked cookies are a fun way to indulge the artist in any kid. Keep a batch of unfrosted cookies in the freezer for up to 2 months; you'll have them on hand for the kids to frost and decorate anytime.

1 Cookie: Calories 100 (Calories from Fat 65); Fat 7g (Saturated 3g); Cholesterol 20mg; Sodium 160mg; Carbohydrate 8g (Dietary Fiber 0g); Protein 1g • **% Daily Value:** Vitamin A 2%; Vitamin C 0%; Calcium 2%; Iron 2% • **Exchanges:** 1/2 Starch, 1 1/2 Fat • **Carbohydrate Choices:** 1/2

Ultimate Sugar Cookie Cut-Ups

Lickety-Split Gingersnaps

PREP: 15 MIN; BAKE: 15 MIN PER SHEET; COOL: 35 MIN

About 4 dozen cookies

1 cup packed dark brown sugar

1/3 cup shortening

1/4 cup full-flavor molasses

1 egg

2 1/2 cups Original Bisquick mix

1 1/2 teaspoons ground allspice

1 1/2 teaspoons ground ginger

2 tablespoons granulated sugar

1. Heat oven to 375°. Mix brown sugar, shortening, molasses and egg in large bowl with spoon. Stir in Bisquick mix, allspice and ginger. Place dough on surface generously dusted with Bisquick mix; gently roll in Bisquick mix to coat.

2. Divide dough into 4 parts. Shape each part into roll 3/4 to 1 inch in diameter and about 12 inches long. Place rolls about 2 inches apart on large ungreased cookie sheet. Sprinkle granulated sugar down centers of rolls.

3. Bake 12 to 15 minutes or until set and slightly cracked. Cool on cookie sheet 5 minutes. Cut diagonally into about 1-inch strips. Carefully remove from cookie sheet to wire rack. Cool completely, about 30 minutes.

High Altitude (3500 to 6500 feet): Use 1/4 cup shortening. Bake 2 rolls on 1 sheet at a time 12 to 14 minutes.

Betty's **TIP:** No allspice? Spice it up with 1 teaspoon ground cinnamon and 1/2 teaspoon ground cloves. Drizzle gingersnaps with melted white baking chips when you want an extra-special look.

1 Cookie: Calories 60 (Calories from Fat 20); Fat 2g (Saturated 1g); Cholesterol 5mg; Sodium 90mg; Carbohydrate 10g (Dietary Fiber 0g); Protein 1g • **% Daily Value:** Vitamin A 0%; Vitamin C 0%; Calcium 2%; Iron 2% • **Exchanges:** 1/2 Starch, 1/2 Fat • **Carbohydrate Choices:** 1/2

Lickety-Split Gingersnaps

Brown Sugar Drops

PREP: 12 MIN; BAKE: 10 MIN PER SHEET; COOL: 20 MIN

About 3 1/2 dozen cookies

1 1/4 cups packed brown sugar

1/4 cup butter or margarine, softened

1/4 cup shortening (or softened butter or margarine)

1 teaspoon vanilla

2 eggs

3 1/2 cups Original Bisquick mix

Browned Butter Frosting (below)

Browned Butter Frosting

1/3 cup butter or margarine

3 cups powdered sugar

1 1/2 teaspoons vanilla

3 to 4 tablespoons milk

1. Heat oven to 375°. Mix all ingredients except Bisquick mix and Browned Butter Frosting in large bowl with spoon. Stir in Bisquick mix until blended.

2. Drop dough by rounded teaspoonfuls about 2 inches apart onto ungreased cookie sheet.

3. Bake 8 to 10 minutes until light golden brown. Remove from cookie sheet to wire rack. Cool completely, about 20 minutes. Frost with Browned Butter Frosting.

Browned Butter Frosting

Heat butter in 3-quart saucepan over medium-high heat just until light brown; remove from heat. Stir in powdered sugar, vanilla and enough milk to make frosting smooth and spreadable.

High Altitude (3500 to 6500 feet): Bake 9 to 11 minutes.

Betty's **TIP:** For a fancy finish, top each frosted cookie with a pecan half. If you don't have time to make frosting from scratch, use a 16-ounce tub of dulce de leche (caramel) ready-to-spread frosting instead.

1 Cookie: Calories 135 (Calories from Fat 45); Fat 5g (Saturated 2g); Cholesterol 15mg; Sodium 0mg; Carbohydrate 21g (Dietary Fiber 0g); Protein 1g • **% Daily Value:** Vitamin A 2%; Vitamin C 0%; Calcium 2%; Iron 2% • **Exchanges:** 1/2 Starch, 1 Other Carbohydrate, 1 Fat • **Carbohydrate Choices:** 1 1/2

Saucepan Granola Bars

PREP: 10 MIN; BAKE: 25 MIN; COOL: 1 HR

48 bars

1/2 cup butter or margarine

2 1/2 cups Original Bisquick mix

2 cups granola with fruit

1 cup packed brown sugar

1/2 cup chopped nuts

1 teaspoon vanilla

2 eggs

1. Heat oven to 375°. Melt butter in 3-quart saucepan over low heat. Stir in remaining ingredients until blended. Spoon into ungreased rectangular pan, 13 × 9 × 2 inches; spread evenly.

2. Bake 20 to 25 minutes or until deep golden brown. Cool completely, about 1 hour. For bars, cut into 8 rows by 6 rows.

High Altitude (3500 to 6500 feet): Bake 23 to 27 minutes.

Betty's **TIP:** For a special touch, package individual bars in plastic wrap and gift a trail buff with these brown sugary treats.

1 Bar: Calories 85 (Calories from Fat 35); Fat 4g (Saturated 2g); Cholesterol 15mg; Sodium 130mg; Carbohydrate 11g (Dietary Fiber 0g); Protein 1g • **% Daily Value:** Vitamin A 2%; Vitamin C 0%; Calcium 2%; Iron 2% • **Exchanges:** 1/2 Starch, 1/2 Other Carbohydrate, 1/2 Fat • **Carbohydrate Choices:** 1

Rum-Raisin Bars

PREP: 15 MIN; BAKE: 16 MIN; COOL: 30 MIN

4 dozen bars

1 cup raisins

3/4 cup water

3/4 cup granulated sugar

1/2 cup butter or margarine

1 3/4 cups Original Bisquick mix

1 1/2 teaspoons rum extract

1 egg

Rum Glaze (below)

Rum Glaze

3/4 cup powdered sugar

1 tablespoon butter or margarine, melted

3 to 4 teaspoons milk

1/2 teaspoon rum extract

1. Heat oven to 350°. Grease bottom and sides of rectangular pan, 13 × 9 × 2 inches, with shortening or spray with cooking spray. Heat raisins and water to boiling in 2-quart saucepan over medium-high heat. Boil 5 minutes, stirring occasionally. Immediately remove from heat; drain any remaining liquid. Add sugar and butter to raisins. Cool 5 minutes, stirring occasionally, until butter is melted.

2. Stir Bisquick mix, rum extract and egg into raisin mixture until blended. Spoon batter into pan; spread evenly.

3. Bake 15 to 16 minutes or until golden brown and toothpick inserted in center comes out clean. Spoon Rum Glaze over warm bars; spread evenly. Cool completely, about 30 minutes. For bars, cut into 8 rows by 6 rows.

Rum Glaze
Stir all ingredients until smooth and spreadable.

High Altitude (3500 to 6500 feet): Use 1/2 cup granulated sugar and 1/4 cup butter.

Betty's **TIP:** These grown-up treats are so easy to bake and take to your next office party. Not a fan of rum? Use vanilla in place of the rum extract.

1 Bar: Calories 70 (Calories from Fat 25); Fat 3g (Saturated 2g); Cholesterol 10mg; Sodium 80mg; Carbohydrate 10g (Dietary Fiber 0g); 1Protein g • **% Daily Value:** Vitamin A 2%; Vitamin C 0%; Calcium 0%; Iron 0% • **Exchanges:** 1/2 Starch, 1/2 Fat • **Carbohydrate Choices:** 1/2

Rum-Raisin Bars

ULTIMATE Triple-Chocolate Bars

PREP: 15 MIN; BAKE: 35 MIN; COOL: 1 HR; CHILL: 1 HR

4 dozen bars

1 bag (12 ounces) semisweet chocolate chips (2 cups)

2 packages (3 ounces each) cream cheese

2/3 cup evaporated milk

2 cups Original Bisquick mix

3/4 cup sugar

1/2 cup baking cocoa

3/4 cup butter or margarine, softened

1 cup white baking chips

1 bag (6 ounces) semisweet chocolate chips (1 cup)

1. Heat oven to 375°. Heat 2 cups chocolate chips, the cream cheese and milk in 2-quart saucepan over low heat, stirring constantly, until chips are melted and mixture is smooth. Cool while making crust.

2. Mix Bisquick mix, sugar and cocoa in medium bowl. Cut in butter, using pastry blender or crisscrossing 2 knives, until mixture is crumbly. Press half of the crumbly mixture (2 cups) on bottom of ungreased rectangular pan, 13 × 9 × 2 inches. Sprinkle with white baking chips. Spoon chocolate mixture over crumbly mixture and chips; spread evenly. Sprinkle with remaining crumbly mixture and 1 cup chocolate chips. Press lightly with fork.

3. Bake 30 to 35 minutes until center is set. Cool completely, about 1 hour. Refrigerate 1 hour until chilled. For bars, cut into 8 rows by 6 rows. Store covered in refrigerator.

High Altitude (3500 to 6500 feet): No changes.

Betty's **TIP:** Surprise a chocolate lover with these decadent bars baked in a disposable pan. Add 1/2 cup chopped walnuts or pecans with the white baking chips for an extra indulgence.

1 Bar: Calories 165 (Calories from Fat 90); Fat 10g (Saturated 6g); Cholesterol 15mg; Sodium 110mg; Carbohydrate 17g (Dietary Fiber 1g); Protein 2g • % **Daily Value:** Vitamin A 4%; Vitamin C 0%; Calcium 4%; Iron 4% • **Exchanges:** 1 Starch, 2 Fat • **Carbohydrate Choices:** 1

Ultimate Triple-Chocolate Bars

Peanutty Cream Bars

PREP: 14 MIN; BAKE: 20 MIN; CHILL: 2 HR

25 bars

1 1/4 cups Original Bisquick mix

1/2 cup powdered sugar

1/4 cup firm butter or margarine

1 tablespoon hot water

3/4 cup whipping (heavy) cream

1 bag (10 ounces) peanut butter chips (1 2/3 cups)

1/2 cup dry-roasted peanuts

1. Heat oven to 350°. Mix Bisquick mix and powdered sugar in medium bowl. Cut in butter, using pastry blender or crisscrossing 2 knives, until mixture is crumbly. Stir in hot water. Press mixture firmly on bottom of ungreased 8 × 8 × 2 or 9 × 9 × 2-inch square pan.

2. Bake 15 to 20 minutes or until set and golden brown around edges.

3. Heat whipping cream and peanut butter chips in 1-quart saucepan over medium heat, stirring constantly, until smooth. Pour over baked crust; spread evenly. Sprinkle with peanuts. Refrigerate at least 2 hours until set. For bars, cut into 5 rows by 5 rows.

High Altitude (3500 to 6500 feet): No changes.

Betty's **TIP:** Drizzle these ultra nutty bars with melted semisweet chocolate for a decadent finish. Or cut bars into candy-size pieces and place in paper candy cups for serving.

1 Bar: Calories 155 (Calories from Fat 90); Fat 10g (Saturated 4g); Cholesterol 15mg; Sodium 155mg; Carbohydrate 13g (Dietary Fiber 1g); Protein 3g • **% Daily Value:** Vitamin A 2%; Vitamin C 0%; Calcium 2%; Iron 2% • **Exchanges:** 1 Starch, 1 1/2 Fat • **Carbohydrate Choices:** 1

Peanutty Cream Bars

Extreme Bars

PREP: 10 MIN; BAKE: 18 MIN; COOL: 1 HR

25 bars

2 cups Original Bisquick mix

1 cup powdered sugar

1/2 cup butter or margarine, softened

1 egg

1 package (about 0.13 ounce) strawberry-, lemon-, orange- or lime-flavored unsweetened soft drink mix

1 cup vanilla ready-to-spread frosting (from 16-ounce tub)

Candy sprinkles, fruit-flavored gummy ring-shaped candies, gumdrops or jelly beans, if desired

1. Heat oven to 350°. Mix Bisquick mix, powdered sugar, butter, egg and drink mix (dry) in medium bowl with spoon until dough forms. Pat mixture firmly on bottom of ungreased square pan, 8 × 8 × 2 inches.

2. Bake 14 to 18 minutes or until lightly browned around edges. Cool in pan on wire rack about 1 hour.

3. Spread bars with frosting; sprinkle with candies. For bars, cut into 5 rows by 5 rows.

High Altitude (3500 to 6500 feet): Heat oven to 375°. Use 1/4 cup butter. Bake 16 to 18 minutes.

Betty's **TIP:** Neon red, orange and green bars are some of your color options, depending on the soft-drink mix you choose. These bars are great at birthday time; decorate the top with gummy candy rings for handy birthday candleholders.

1 Bar: Calories 145 (Calories from Fat 65); Fat 7g (Saturated 4g); Cholesterol 20mg; Sodium 70mg; Carbohydrate 20g (Dietary Fiber 0g); Protein 1g • **% Daily Value:** Vitamin A 2%; Vitamin C 0%; Calcium 2%; Iron 2% • **Exchanges:** 1/2 Starch, 1/2 Other Carbohydrate, 1 1/2 Fat • **Carbohydrate Choices:** 1

Extreme Bars

Helpful Nutrition and Cooking Information

Nutrition Guidelines

We provide nutrition information for each recipe that includes calories, fat, cholesterol, sodium, carbohydrate, fiber and protein. Individual food choices can be based on this information.

Recommended intake for a daily diet of 2,000 calories as set by the Food and Drug Administration		
Total Fat	Less than 65g
Saturated Fat	Less than 20g
Cholesterol	Less than 300mg
Sodium	Less than 2,400mg
Total Carbohydrate	300g
Dietary Fiber	25g

Criteria Used for Calculating Nutrition Information

- The first ingredient was used wherever a choice is given (such as 1/3 cup sour cream or plain yogurt).
- The first ingredient amount was used wherever a range is given (such as 3- to 3 1/2-pound cut-up broiler-fryer chicken).
- The first serving number was used wherever a range is given (such as 4 to 6 servings).
- "If desired" ingredients and recipe variations were not included (such as sprinkle with brown sugar, if desired).
- Only the amount of a marinade or frying oil that is estimated to be absorbed by the food during preparation or cooking was calculated.

Ingredients Used in Recipe Testing and Nutrition Calculations

- Ingredients used for testing represent those that the majority of consumers use in their homes: large eggs, 2% milk, 80%-lean ground beef, canned ready-to-use chicken broth and vegetable oil spread containing not less than 65 percent fat.
- Fat-free, low-fat or low-sodium products were not used, unless otherwise indicated.
- Solid vegetable shortening (not butter, margarine, nonstick cooking sprays or vegetable oil spread as they can cause sticking problems) was used to grease pans, unless otherwise indicated.

Equipment Used in Recipe Testing

We use equipment for testing that the majority of consumers use in their homes. If a specific piece of equipment (such as a wire whisk) is necessary for recipe success, it is listed in the recipe.

- Cookware and bakeware without nonstick coatings were used, unless otherwise indicated.
- No dark-colored, black or insulated bakeware was used.
- When a pan is specified in a recipe, a metal pan was used; a baking dish or pie plate means ovenproof glass was used.
- An electric hand mixer was used for mixing only when mixer speeds are specified in the recipe directions. When a mixer speed is not given, a spoon or fork was used.

Cooking Terms Glossary

Beat: Mix ingredients vigorously with spoon, fork, wire whisk, hand beater or electric mixer until smooth and uniform.

Boil: Heat liquid until bubbles rise continuously and break on the surface and steam is given off. For rolling boil, the bubbles form rapidly.

Chop: Cut into coarse or fine irregular pieces with a knife, food chopper, blender or food processor.

Cube: Cut into squares 1/2 inch or larger.

Dice: Cut into squares smaller than 1/2 inch.

Grate: Cut into tiny particles using small rough holes of grater (citrus peel or chocolate).

Grease: Rub the inside surface of a pan with shortening, using pastry brush, piece of waxed paper or paper towel, to prevent food from sticking during baking (as for some casseroles).

Julienne: Cut into thin, matchlike strips, using knife or food processor (vegetables, fruits, meats).

Mix: Combine ingredients in any way that distributes them evenly.

Sauté: Cook foods in hot oil over medium-high heat with frequent tossing and turning motion.

Shred: Cut into long thin pieces by rubbing food across the holes of a shredder, as for cheese, or by using a knife to slice very thinly, as for cabbage.

Simmer: Cook in liquid just below the boiling point on top of the stove, usually after reducing heat from a boil. Bubbles will rise slowly and break just below the surface.

Stir: Mix ingredients until uniform consistency. Stir once in a while for stirring occasionally, often for stirring frequently and continuously for stirring constantly.

Toss: Tumble ingredients (such as green salad) lightly with a lifting motion, usually to coat evenly or mix with another food.

Metric Conversion Guide

Volume

U.S. Units	Canadian Metric	Australian Metric
1/4 teaspoon	1 mL	1 ml
1/2 teaspoon	2 mL	2 ml
1 teaspoon	5 mL	5 ml
1 tablespoon	15 mL	20 ml
1/4 cup	50 mL	60 ml
1/3 cup	75 mL	80 ml
1/2 cup	125 mL	125 ml
2/3 cup	150 mL	170 ml
3/4 cup	175 mL	190 ml
1 cup	250 mL	250 ml
1 quart	1 liter	1 liter
1 1/2 quarts	1.5 liters	1.5 liters
2 quarts	2 liters	2 liters
2 1/2 quarts	2.5 liters	2.5 liters
3 quarts	3 liters	3 liters
4 quarts	4 liters	4 liters

Weight

U.S. Units	Canadian Metric	Australian Metric
1 ounce	30 grams	30 grams
2 ounces	55 grams	60 grams
3 ounces	85 grams	90 grams
4 ounces (1/4 pound)	115 grams	125 grams
8 ounces (1/2 pound)	225 grams	225 grams
16 ounces (1 pound)	455 grams	500 grams
1 pound	455 grams	1/2 kilogram

The recipes in this cookbook have not been developed or tested using metric measures. When converting recipes to metric, some variations in quality may be noted.

Measurements

Inches	Centimeters
1	2.5
2	5.0
3	7.5
4	10.0
5	12.5
6	15.0
7	17.5
8	20.5
9	23.0
10	25.5
11	28.0
12	30.5
13	33.0

Temperatures

Fahrenheit	Celsius
32°	0°
212°	100°
250°	120°
275°	140°
300°	150°
325°	160°
350°	180°
375°	190°
400°	200°
425°	220°
450°	230°
475°	240°
500°	260°

INDEX

Page numbers in *italics* indicate a photograph.

Complete your cookbook library
with these *Betty Crocker* titles

Betty Crocker's **Best Bread Machine Cookbook**

Betty Crocker's **Best Chicken Cookbook**

Betty Crocker's **Best Christmas Cookbook**

Betty Crocker's **Best of Baking**

Betty Crocker's **Best of Healthy and Hearty Cooking**

Betty Crocker's **Best-Loved Recipes**

Betty Crocker's **Bisquick® Cookbook**

Betty Crocker's **Bread Machine Cookbook**

Betty Crocker's **Ultimate Cake Mix Cookbook**

Betty Crocker's **Cook It Quick**

Betty Crocker's Cookbook, 9th Edition—*The* BIG RED *Cookbook*®

Betty Crocker's **Cookbook, Bridal Edition**

Betty Crocker's **Cook Book for Boys and Girls, Facsimile Edition**

Betty Crocker's **Cookie Book**

Betty Crocker's **Cooking for Two**

Betty Crocker's **Cooky Book, Facsimile Edition**

Betty Crocker's **Cooking Basics**

Betty Crocker's **Diabetes Cookbook**

Betty Crocker's **Easy Slow Cooker Dinners**

Betty Crocker's **Eat and Lose Weight**

Betty Crocker's **Entertaining Basics**

Betty Crocker's **Flavors of Home**

Betty Crocker **Four-Ingredient Cookbook**

Betty Crocker's **Great Grilling**

Betty Crocker's **Healthy New Choices**

Betty Crocker's **Indian Home Cooking**

Betty Crocker's **Italian Cooking**

Betty Crocker's **Kids Cook!**

Betty Crocker's **Kitchen Library**

Betty Crocker's **Living with Cancer Cookbook**

Betty Crocker's **Low-Fat Low-Cholesterol Cooking Today**

Betty Crocker **More Slow Cooker Recipes**

Betty Crocker's **New Cake Decorating**

Betty Crocker's **New Chinese Cookbook**

Betty Crocker's **A Passion for Pasta**

Betty Crocker's **Picture Cook Book, Facsimile Edition**

Betty Crocker's **Quick & Easy Cookbook**

Betty Crocker's **Slow Cooker Cookbook**

Betty Crocker's **Southwest Cooking**

Betty Crocker **Complete Thanksgiving Cookbook**

Betty Crocker's **Vegetarian Cooking**